THE WORD IS PROPHECY

Knowing that God is God and His sovereignty remains in a dark world

Dr Lionel Etan-Adollo

ATHENA PRESS
LONDON

THE WORD IS PROPHECY
Knowing that God is God and His sovereignty remains in a dark world
Copyright © Dr Lionel Etan-Adollo 2003

All Rights Reserved

No part of this book may be reproduced in any form
by photocopying or by any electronic or mechanical means,
including information storage and retrieval systems,
without permission in writing from both the copyright
owner and the publisher of this book.

ISBN 1 84401 117 8

Published 2003 by
ATHENA PRESS
Queen's House, 2 Holly Road
Twickenham TW1 4EG

First Published by
AVON BOOKS
1 Dovedale Studios
465 Battersea Park Road
London sw11 4LR

Printed for Athena Press

THE WORD IS PROPHECY
Knowing that God is God and His sovereignty remains in a dark world

Acknowledgements

With profound love I would like to acknowledge and thank the brethren who attended the Sunday sermon and the presentation of excerpts from this book on November 5, 1995 at 'The Way Fellowship – Hyde Park', London. I say thank you for your support and God bless you all.

I would also like to put on record the event of the assassination of President Yitshak Rabin of Israel on the eve of the presentation of this work. It is my wish and fervent prayer that the future Israel will bring the nation of Israel closer to God.

*Dedicated to HIM who is TRUTH,
and all those ones all over the world who live for Truth in a fast-changing world.*

The Word of God, the Truth, is absolute, and the appreciation of the Truth revealed in the Word amongst men has always been progressive.

To my grandmother, Emmanuella Agboola Ogunmuyiwa (1913–90), a fervent Christian with sound Christian ethics, an amiable Educator and an award-winner who planted many Christian schools and supported the Church and the Red Cross, amongst other charitable works, all over Nigeria and West Africa. A woman of great mind, vision, purpose, excellence and character, indeed of such that inspires great men and legends.

I miss you very much Grandma!

An Ode on Dogma, Knowledge and God

Dogma stifles the body, soul and spirit
Dogma stifles the Word of God
Dogma stifles the world and its possible inquisitions
Dogma stifles the possibilities of God in man and for the world
Dogma stifles the Church and the love of Christ for His own
Dogma stifles the freedom and liberty assured through the blood of Christ.

For God is the Author of the heavens and the earth
And Christ the Centre of His throne
For Christ has given freely of His wisdom and knowledge
And knowledge that is beyond religion
For Christ cannot be compartmentalized – He is One and All
And Copernicus, Galileo, Pascal, Kepler and Newton were early Christians who were also scientists
For I see God in Physics, Chemistry, Music, Mathematics, History, Art and in all faculties
And Christ revealed I know is the source of all faculties – the giver of ingenuity
For Christ can be proven and related to all faculties and humanist professions of men
And Christ has given all knowledge unto men in which religion is one
For He – the source of all knowledge – His domain is beyond religious dogma
And Christ has freely given His knowledge – His light – to shine the world For the use of His own, and for His glorification.

Believers, arise in God's power and rule the faculties and the world
Believe, it is Christ who makes the earth revolve
Believers, believe western civilization is a product of Christian tradition
Believers, believe science is a product of Christianity
Believers, believe – for it is written the Maker has made all and has authority over all
Believers, believe – for it is written the Redeemer has conquered and given all treasures unto those who believe in Him
Believers, believe the truth is one and the source is Christ.

For let us agree as it is written – all creation must come to Jesus, for all things have been committed to Him by His Father including all wisdom and knowledge
And let us agree as it is written – the earth is the Lord's and everything in it, the world and all who live in it. Faith and reason are from one source – God
For God is the author and owner of creative talents
And Christ is beyond religion – He governs all faculties of nature and man
For God-man covenant is beyond religion – it governs all faculties of man and existence.

Contents

Acknowledgement	v
Dedication	vii
An Ode on Dogma, Knowledge and God	xi
1.0 Purpose of Study	17
1.1 Twenty-four statements and questions that establish the purpose of this book	17
1.2 Why I write the way I do	24
2.0 Prologue	27
2.1 Exaltation of God's Sovereignty	27
3.0 The Word is Prophecy	30
3.1 Impact of Bible Studies	30
3.2 Personal Revelation of God's Word (knowledge that God is God, and His sovereignty remains in a dark world	31
4.0 Prophecy	45
5.0 The Prophecy Box	48
5.1 Description of the model	50
(i) God's Love	50
(ii) The Word, or any of the names associated with God in three persons (God the Father, God the Son and God the Holy Spirit)	51
(iii) Genesis to Revelation (i.e. Word of God/ the Holy Bible)	53

(iv)	The Theory of Prophecy	53
(v)	The Spirit Realm and the Physical Realm	53
(vi)	The Heavens and the Earth	53
(vii)	The Preparation Model	54
(viii)	The Visualisation and Realisation Experience	56
(ix)	The Reductive and Restoration Experience	57
(x)	The Deep Theory	58
(xi)	The Gospel Truth Model	60
(xii)	The Old and the New Testament are One and Continuous	61
(xiii)	God's Faith (or zeal)	61
(xiv)	Jesus is the Light shining in the dark place	62
(xv)	The Master's Call	63
(xvi)	The Christian's Life Experience (Christ's experience on earth)	64
(xvii)	The Prophet's Experience	65
(xviii)	The Concept of Judgement	66
(xix)	Spiritual location of the Word of God	67
(xx)	Rebuking and Training process	69
(xxi)	Timing and Consistency	69
(xxii)	Prophecy is about Testimony	70
(xxiii)	Prophets	71
(xxiv)	False personal Prophecies	72
(xxv)	Concept of Continuity	74
(xxvi)	Literature and Prophecy Compared	75
(xxvii)	The Word is Prophecy	75

6.0 The Prophecy Box Further Elaborated and Tested — 78

6.1 Method of Visualisation and Realisation — 78

6.2 Method of Reduction and Restoration		81
(I)	Restoration	81
(II)	Reduction	82
6.3 Why are we reduced?		82
6.4 How do we deal with reductive prophecies?		83
(I)	Word of God	83
(II)	Meditation	83
(III)	The Human Body as the Temple of God	84
(IV)	Prayer	84
(V)	Praise and Worship	85
(VI)	Fasting	85
(VII)	Healing and Deliverance	88
6.5 When will there be an end to reduction (discomfort, discouragement, deception and conflict)?		90
Epilogue		92
Bibliography		95

1.0 Purpose of Study

1.1 TWENTY-FOUR STATEMENTS AND QUESTIONS THAT ESTABLISH THE PURPOSE OF THIS BOOK

This book, *The Word is Prophecy*, gives answers to twenty-four statements and questions we may ask as Christians in a study such as this on *Prophecy*. The description of *The Prophecy Box* (p.48) also provides answers. The twenty-four statements and questions, which establish the purpose of this study, are:

(i) How does the analogy of the heavens and the earth within the universe prove the existence of God?

(ii) How do we prove and establish the authority of God and His supremacy in the heavens and on earth?

(iii) How do we prove the story of creation beginning with the creation of the heavens and the earth?

(iv) How do we prove coherently the authenticity of God in three persons and God as one (that is, the analogy of God the Father, God the Son and God the Holy Spirit, that they are distinct and the same)?

(v) How do we prove the authenticity of the Holy Scriptures (that is, the Holy Bible or the word of God from Genesis to Revelation)?

(vi) As distinct as the various books in the Bible are, is the Holy Bible an un-integrated whole? It is proven in this work that the Holy Bible is an integrated whole through the treatise expressed in *The Prophecy Box*.

(vii) In the midst of aridity of life (for instance, the thousands of lives lost on 9-11 at the World Trade Center, New York, the millions of Jews killed in Nazi camps during the Second World War amongst many disasters and wars the world has witnessed), how do we establish the sovereignty of God over creation?

(viii) Since the death of Jesus Christ over two thousand years ago and with the state of the world now, can we trace events we observe daily to the word of God?

(ix) Why sin, and what are the results of the fall of man?

(x) Is it true that sin and the fall of man are the causes of *reduction* (for instance, humiliation, disgrace, failure) of the human race? Is it true that the process of *reduction* to *restoration* is a method of operation by God with man? Is it true that the sovereignty of God over all circumstance and events in our life and world guarantees *restoration* (that is replacement of that which is lost to the devil and elevation to greater heights not attained in the original state of events and circumstance)?

(xi) Does this theme *reduction* to *restoration* encompass the whole of the Biblical stories and key personalities? Was the Biblical nation of Israel reduced and then restored? What of Abraham, Jacob (later named Israel), Isaac, Joseph, Daniel, David, Jesus Christ, Paul, Peter, and all in the Biblical roll of honour named in Hebrew 11?

(xii) Can this theme of reduction to restoration sum up the entire experience in the word of God from Genesis to Revelation and the Christian's life? Yes, I believe so, and this is frankly proven in *The Word is Prophecy*.

(xiii) What other theme in the Holy Scriptures encompasses the whole nature of God? Is it *Prophecy*? Yes, I believe so and this is frankly proven in this book.

(xiv) What is *Prophecy*? Is the entire word of God from Genesis to Revelation *Prophecy*? Yes. Can we therefore define *Prophecy* in a *broader context* as the word of God (for instance, the entire written word of God from Genesis to Revelation)? Yes. Intuitively, can we say *Prophecy in a broader context,* as defined above, does supersede *personal prophecy*? Yes. What is personal *prophecy*? Is it spoken word given by God instantaneously through His Prophets and other avenues (for instance, through personal vision and dreams)? Is it still true today? Does personal *prophecy* add to the Holy Scriptures? No, the Scriptures are inerrant and true. Is it true that *personal prophecy* must be subject to the Holy Scriptures? Yes. Does it therefore mean that *personal prophecy,* as suggested above, must be subject to the definition of *Prophecy as defined in the broader context*? To all the unanswered questions above, my answer is Yes, and this is proven in this book.

(xv) How dynamic is the theme and definition of *Prophecy in the broader context*? See *The Prophecy Box* and the analogy of God the Father, God the Son and God the Holy Spirit.

(xvi) Is it true that the word of God cannot be separated from the Christian foundational truth and acceptance of faith in God the Father, God the Son and God the Holy Spirit, and that each of the three persons can be equated to the word of God? Yes. Therefore, if truly *Prophecy* in the broader context is the word of God, can it also

1.0 Purpose of Study

be God-personified? *Is it possible to say Prophecy in the broader context represents God the Father, God the Son and God the Holy Spirit? Can we therefore say that the term 'Prophecy' in the broader context could mean the Trinity and each of the three persons?*

(xvii) How has sin and the fall of man radically presented the subject of *Prophecy*[1]? Is man and the Christian's earthly experience and existence not a reflection of the word of God from Genesis to Revelation and Christ's earthly experience? Paul says about *personal prophecies*, 'He who prophesies speaks to men for their upbuilding and encouragement and consolation' (1 Cor. 14: 3). How does this fit into the global definition of *Prophecy in the broader context*? Is it not also true that the message we read from the written word of God of *Prophecy* is about sin of man and redemption/salvation through Jesus Christ? Is the written word of God of *Prophecy* not laced with the theme of *reduction* and *restoration*? How many men of God were not humiliated and re-established and elevated?

(xviii) How do the two themes *reduction* to *restoration* and the written word of God of *Prophecy* equate? Do the two themes together focus on the pattern of God, and on the pattern of man's existence throughout life? What do the two themes say about the Christian's life? Does the Christian's life fall into this pattern?

(xix) What are *positive prophecy* and *reductive prophecy*, and why *positive prophesy* and *reductive prophecy*? Does *positive prophecy* reveal God's perfection? Yes. Does *reductive prophecy* present God as lesser?

---

[1] As we proceed whenever I say *Prophecy*, I mean *Prophecy as defined in a broader context*, and whenever I mean *personal prophecy* I will state that categorically. Therefore, the terms *Prophecy* and *Prophecy in the broader context* refer to the same event and are used interchangeably throughout this book.

No, *reduction* must lead to *restoration* that is part of the plan of God and why Jesus Christ died for all and He is still coming back to gather His own.

(xx) What is the importance of being *holy*, and how does it bring us nearer to God, and is it true it is the key to all God's blessings? What are the fruits of being *holy*? What are the *holy standards of God*?

(xxi) What fundamental message do we learn about *Faith* (for instance, through God's faith in His word in His act of creation of the heavens and the earth)?

(xxii) Is it true God says He is *Love*? Yes. What is *love*? What do we understand by *God's love*? Is love supreme to being *holy*? No, they are distinct and inseparable. *When we refer to God regarding the two terms, we remember God saying He is Holy and the fact that the written word of God from Genesis to Revelation is called the Holy Bible and not Love Bible!* What is the nature of the relationship between *love* and being *holy*? Is the relationship between *love* and being *holy* akin to the relationship of God the Father and His Son? Yes. Is it true that at the centre/heart of God's throne is the lamb slain which is Christ and also *Holy*? Yes. Is it also true that at the heart of God is holiness? Yes. Is it therefore true that at the centre/heart of *God's love is Holiness*? Yes. *As we cannot separate God's only begotten Son from the Father, so we cannot separate being holy from love.* What are the barriers to receiving God's love, and also what are the barriers to being holy? Disobedience to the word of God and the holy requirements of God referred to as *The Holy Standards of God*. See further explanation of God's love in the discussion on *The Prophecy Box*. How does Paul's statement that *Prophecy will cease and Love will remain* (1 Cor. 13: 8–13) fit into the global

1.0 Purpose of Study

definition of *Prophecy in the broader context*? I believe Paul was referring to *personal prophecies*, and *personal prophecy will indeed cease (and not Prophecy in the broader context*) when Jesus Christ comes back and/or as we bring heaven down to earth through prayer (Matt. 6: 10). *The Word of God of Prophecy from Genesis to Revelation is eternal and will not cease, so also His Love who is God.*

(xxiii) Who is Abraham? Who are the seeds of Abraham and the children of the promise? Who is Isaac? Who is Jacob? Why was he called *Israel*? What is the significance of the name *Israel* in the Old Testament? What are the old covenant and the new covenant? What is the link between the two covenants? Is it right to call Christian-believers under the new covenant the *New Israel*, that is, as those entitled and assured of an inheritance and the glorious riches of God? I do. Is it right to categorize the Old Testament Israel and the New Testament benefactors (that is Christian-believers) as *Israel* as I did earlier? I do[1]. Is it still true that God's first love is *Israel*, with which He established the first cord in the Old Testament? Is it still true that God's ancient cord with *Israel* has not changed and, '...the gifts and the call of God are irrevocable' as Paul said concerning the status of the Jewish people with God in Romans 11: 29? Is the *New Israel*[2] not sharing in the

---

[1] Indeed, literally and spiritually, I find it convenient for the purposes of this book. A strange fashion it will seem to some readers. I hope readers will understand that this method is intentional. There is therefore need for discernment sometimes to understand which Israel I am specifically speaking about in the Prologue and Epilogue chapters. For clearer meaning, most times when the name Israel is in italic (in the Prologue and Epilogue chapters) I am referring to both Old Testament Israel and New Testament benefactors of the covenant.

[2] New Testament believers of the Christian faith are referred to as the *New Israel* (Romans 9: 23–26; Hebrews 8: 7–13; 1 Peter 2: 9–10). The terms *Israel* and *New Israel* are used interchangeably for Christian believers in this book.

inheritance of the old *Israel*? What is God's master plan and purpose for the old *Israel* and the New Israel? What is the importance of the first cord with old *Israel*? Is it not true that both the Old Testament and the New Testament are a *continuous* story? Yes. Is this *continuous* story separable from the analogy of God the Father, God the Son and God the Holy Spirit? No, see *The Prophecy Box*. How relevant is the Old Testament *Israel* to the scheme of things in the New Testament?

(xxiv) Is it true that the earth is the Lord's and all therein? Yes. What about humanist professions, can we find God therein? Yes. Is God the author of ingenuity and the source of all creative talents and human reason? Yes. Who created all that is seen and unseen both in the physical and in the spiritual? God. How much control does the devil have in the heavens, the earth and in the minds of men? How far can the devil go? Who shall stand to the end? Who shall triumph over the enemy? Those ready to live according to the holy standards of God laid down in the Holy Scriptures, and above all, those assured of God's presence, mercy and grace, which is sufficient.

In the first category, if some of these statements/questions raised and answers given in this book do not take you back to the Holy Scriptures for further enquiry (or do not seem *controversial* and *challenging* enough), then this book is not meant for you and has not served its purpose.

In the second category, if this level of theological and biblical abstraction meets your personal quest of *knowing who God* is in a more serious and analytical way, then this book has achieved a noble goal.

Ultimately, I pray for you and I will personally derive greater joy if we were challenged to study and know the word of God the way we have never known it before after reading this book.

1.0 Purpose of Study

Happy reading, if you will be going any further than this chapter!

1.2 WHY I WRITE THE WAY I DO

As a Christian-writer, Pastoral Minister and teacher, what do I intend to achieve through this kind of writing and teaching?

(i) I intend to present and teach the Holy Scriptures as an integrated-whole, and in an orderly and systematic fashion from Genesis to Revelation under the inspiration of the Holy Spirit.

(ii) I intend to impart sound Scriptural reasoning and excellence that will lie at the cutting edge of the writing and teaching.

(iii) I am called presently into a well-articulated writing, teaching and publishing ministry that I believe is able to re-orientate the presentation of the Christian-faith from pre-primary school beyond post-graduate school through my peculiar model and blueprint on the *Analogy of the Trinity*, centring all discussion on Church interests (that is *the square-box representing God the Father; the circle in the centre representing Jesus Christ and the Holy Spirit permeating all areas and the four corners of the model*). In this book this model and blueprint is adapted to our subject of interest – that is *The Word is Prophecy* and is called *The Prophecy Box* (p.48).

(iv) For someone baptised as a Catholic at birth, confirmed as an Anglican, Charismatic in the manner of worship and non-denominational at heart, but Christ-focused and one body of Christ inclined, I intend to minister, teach and write for the Church and to proclaim an understanding of God which is in contrast to the simple study of God. That study which is confined to *give me… give me, Lord*, but to broaden minds and propel the individual to in-depth and fundamental knowledge and study of *knowing God* for what He says He is, as the true and only one God of creation (and in three persons God the Father, God the Son and God the Holy Spirit) at all times. I will not consider my writing *soft* and an easy read by popular standards, but educational and serious for those who would like to know more about God.

(v) I intend to add, through a unique flare of style of writing and treatise, in-depth and transcendental Scriptural understanding, knowledge, value and substance to Christian doctrine and ethics in society and in the world under the inspiration of the Holy Spirit. I intend to broaden and stretch the thinking of my readers about the study and understanding of God by the grace of the Holy Spirit. I firmly believe in the inerrancy and infallibility of the Holy Scriptures from Genesis to Revelation and it is my *prima facie* evidence to attest to this fact. I therefore hope that my work (particularly my models centred around the analogy of the Trinity at this time) will attest to this fact about the Holy Scriptures and therefore stand the test of time in generations to come. I pray it will also generate further discussion, re-interpretation, presentation and interest beyond my present scope. Although whilst writing this book I relied primarily and wholly on the unction, leading and inspiration of the Holy Spirit. Therefore, I will not pride myself as having read or known enough books on Christianity and Theology, but I am earnestly learning. Meanwhile, the more I know, the more I discover I do not know. And I believe this gives the possibility to know more.

(vi) As a qualified Shipbroker, Economist, Software Consultant, Project Management Professional, Pastoral Minister, Writer and qualified theologian and a little bit beyond all this, I would like to follow the line of Luke the Physician, Isaiah the Poet and Politician, Paul the Scholar, Aristotle the

1.0 Purpose of Study

Philosopher, John Stuart Mill the Economist, Blaise Pascal the Mathematician/ Computer inventor and many others, particularly those in the marketplace with multifaceted skills and talents that God has used and will continue to use to light and salt the world. As I grow and develop in the Christian faith, I limit not the possibilities of God into wider ministry and further responsibilities in all areas of life, and I cry out and long for holiness and obedience in all areas of my life and work.

So help me, O God, in Jesus' name and by your Holy Spirit, Amen.

London, 2003
Dr Lionel Etan-Adollo
PhD MTh (Oxon) MA BSc Econs MICS PMP
Email: Lionel@etan-adollo.freeserve.co.uk

2.0 Prologue

2.1 Exaltation of God's Sovereignty

The message of the Holy Bible is an integrated whole, coherent and Holy Spirit-inspired to those to whom the Creator has revealed Himself: It is not religious dogma (unquestionable belief) and doctrine, devoid of reasoning and discernment to those divine understanding has specifically been given to. *The Word is Prophecy* exposits the knowledge of God in a methodical way. It is about *knowing God* in His true and proper context through life-patterns exposited throughout the Holy Bible and still revealed in our everyday individual lives on the face of the earth.

In a world and present age incapacitated by sin and imperfections, God remains who He says He is. *The Word is Prophecy* reveals that *God is God, and His sovereignty remains in a dark world*. For the Holy Spirit-filled Christian, there is spiritual understanding and meaning to events, situations and mysteries of life whereby God's presence and sovereignty is always assured (and there is a way out). Throughout existence, God continues to exert His supremacy, and asserts His over-corning authority over events, situations and mysteries of life, however they may manifest. God's conception and creation of the heavens and the earth remains dynamically Christ-centred[1], and therefore the essence of life on earth by man must remain God-glorifying. All creation (mankind) must accept Jesus Christ[2] and glorify God. Those He chose He called *Israel*[3]. And we will not be far too

---

[1] See *The Prophecy Box* p.48.
[2] We must therefore preach and teach the Gospel of Jesus Christ (Matt. 28: 19–20)
[3] Here *Israel* is referred to as both the Old Testament people of Israel and the New Covenant Israel that is Christians-believers (Romans 9: 23–26; Hebrew 8: 7–13; 1 Peter 2: 9–10)

wrong to consider *Israel* a model of the adversities that could plague man, and *Israel* again we will consider still a model of the blessings, fortune and promises God has endowed His chosen and any chosen people with. Israel is the key to Biblical prophecy.

The living *Word of God* (Jesus Christ), and the written *Word of God* (the holy books from Genesis to Revelation), call unto the *deep*[1] and the very essence of life. Every situation must bring Israel back to the Almighty Jehovah, our Saviour and Provider. For in our darkest hour and moment, the ever consistent shining light of the living God, O Ancient of Days, will remain shining in our darkest circumstance and our dark world. Israel must not forget the first cord and his love, which was God, and the covenant relationship established with the Almighty God. Our Lord is a strong tower – when the righteous run to Him, they are safe (Proverbs 18: 10). For God has always been the cloak of *Israel*.

Every situation must bring *Israel* back to God. In crises and in our darkest moment, *Israel* must draw closer to God, retrace and rediscover the highway of salvation and holiness so as to receive God's mercy, grace, love, true peace, justice and righteousness, which is in Jesus Christ, our Lord and Saviour. Then *Israel*, once again, will be lifted up, restored and elevated. For this has always been the experience and story of Israel from Genesis to Revelation, and would continue to be so, so far as human nature and existence remain in their present form. Analogously, the experience and story of *Israel* has been the typical history of mankind.

O Ancient of Days, the Almighty God will never forget the old but still fresh covenant, promises and blessings associated with obedience that He established with *Israel* (Deut. 28: 1–14). As the creation of God's hands (for instance, the heavens and the earth) are set within the universe, so are His prophecies and word contained in His written word from Genesis to Revelation concerning man and this age set before Him. The written word of Prophecy (that is the word of God from Genesis to Revelation)

---

[1] The word *deep* is not intended to be used arrogantly in this book but in a – spiritual sense, acknowledging the depth of the secret and sacred things of God. The ways of God can be beyond human reasoning unless divine revelation is given and this will involve a measure of spirituality.

and God-inspired personal prophecies must come to pass. It is the word of the Lord: 'For the revelation awaits an appointed time; it speaks of the end and will not prove false. Though it linger, wait for it; it will certainly come and will not delay' (Habakkuk 2: 3).

The written word of God is the Lord Himself personified: an affirmation of His personality. On its truth the heaven and the foundation of the earth were formed and hold firm. The stoic nature of God from Genesis to Revelation and His ever-faithful covenant relationship with *Israel* continually reveal the strength of His faithfulness. The Lord will never forget *Israel*, His first cord and love revealed in the Old Testament, and in the New Testament Christians-believers, that is the chosen one of God and also children of the promise! (Romans 9: 23–26; Hebrew 8: 7–13; 1 Peter 2: 9–10). As Christians we are a peculiar and holy nation set apart for God and His purposes, and to light and salt the ends of the earth in every circumstance and situation, however and wherever dark.

For God is God, and His sovereignty remains in a dark world. That is *The Word is Prophecy*! What has Christianity achieved and can Christians still achieve? I hope as we read this work our knowledge and understanding will be enlightened and broadened in this regard.

3.0 The Word is Prophecy

3.1 IMPACT OF BIBLE STUDIES

I have listed four Bible texts below that were prevalent on my mind as I began to think about the sermon on Prophecy for Sunday November 5, 1995. At the time of preparation for the sermon, they were the four texts always staring me in the face each time I opened my Holy Bible. Although I had no specific reasons for them, and neither do I think they were then of any particular relevance to my sermon I cannot deny the overwhelming impact and influence these Bible texts have made on me in the preparation of the sermon, and throughout the writing of this book. The impact made and knowledge gained from the texts is unrelated to the revelation in the letter of each Bible text, but in the general assertions of the four Bible texts:

(i) That any viable discussion about the word of God must be Christ-centred and God glorifying[1].
(ii) That every situation and inexplicable event in life must draw us back to God because only He has the secret answers to all things and mysteries[2].

The result of this book therefore cannot be disassociated from these two general assertions and underlining reasoning of these four Bible texts below. These two assertions and reasonings permeate the whole of this book.

---

[1] In this chapter, *The Word is Prophecy*, it is proven that underlying this reasoning and sentence is the fact that *God is God*. He is who He says He is. His names and triune personality are true.

[2] Underlying this sentence and this entire book *The Word is Prophecy* is the fundamental belief and truth about God that *His sovereignty remains in this dark world*.

The Bible texts are:

(i) John 1: 1–5: 'In the beginning was the Word, and the Word was with God, and the Word was God. He was with God in the beginning. Through Him all things were made; without Him nothing was made that has been made. In Him was life, and that life was the light of men. The light shines in the darkness, but the darkness has not understood it'.

(ii) 1 John 4: 1–2: '…This is how you can recognise the Spirit of God: Every spirit that acknowledges that Jesus Christ has come in the flesh is from God, but every spirit that does not acknowledge Jesus is not from God'.

(iii) Hosea 14: 3: '…O Lord, you show mercy to those who have no one else to turn to'.

(iv) Jeremiah 33: 3: 'Call to me and I will answer you and tell you great and unsearchable things you do not know'.

As I pondered on these four Bible texts, I had a spiritual breakthrough and personal encounter of God's own words on *Prophecy*. That personal revelation led to the title of my sermon and this book, *The Word is Prophecy*.

3.2 PERSONAL REVELATION OF GOD'S WORD
(KNOWLEDGE THAT GOD IS GOD, AND HIS SOVEREIGNTY REMAINS IN A DARK WORLD)

Whilst I am about discussing my personal revelation of God's word on *Prophecy* and who God says He is, neither would I like to wander too far from a wider picture of events at this period relating to my personal life as I remain engrossed with the concerns of my Maker, a sermon and book such as this. I consider myself as a man open and still searching to know more about God, and willing by His grace to draw nearer to Him. I do not count myself as a Biblical authority but a colt striving to be wholly

3.0 The Word is Prophecy

available by His grace for the Master's purposes. I thank God for this season in my life. It was in a season whilst I was engrossed with issues of personal destiny that I had to prepare this sermon. Invariably, in no way can I objectively say that what I now know and have learnt in this season of trying to discover God's perfect will for my life is not intertwined with the preparation of this sermon. I believe the results are still justifiable. Of how much use is any revelation of the Word to a Minister of the Word if what he receives does not bless him, nor address his own concerns? I am sure this book will richly bless those coming from where I am coming from. And those not familiar with my path, they will have something new to learn.

From my encounter, *Prophecy*, I strongly believe, is *God Himself personified*[1], and that is deep. For instance, every man created by God possesses different peculiarities. And as every man is peculiar so are all *personal prophecies*[2]. Therefore, if we can understand all the peculiarities in the 6 billion people of the world, we must be close to understanding the fullness of God and all His *personal prophecies*! I cannot, therefore, say that all I now know is conclusive on the subject of *Prophecy*. However, what I know on *Prophecy* is broader in scope than *personal prophecies*. It relates to prophetic patterns, concepts and methods rather than the subject of personal prophecies. The fact that my revelation has not specifically addressed the subject of personal prophecies, that is not to say that it is not relevant to the understanding of personal prophecies. It behoves me, therefore, to say the Lord has only revealed a broader concept of prophecy and prophetic patterns to me but not the specifics as it relates to individuals. But central to these prophetic patterns and concepts is God, still reigning over all.

God reigns over all His creation and affairs. The sovereignty of God in every event and instant in life cannot be usurped, it is forever settled. No matter how inexplicable a situation may present itself, the goodness of God cannot be taken away from

---

[1] Particularly when it is devoid of satanic influence and attack.
[2] Wayne Grudem defines the gift of prophecy (what I refer to as *personal prophecy*) as *'telling something that God has spontaneously brought to mind'* (*Systematic Theology: An Introduction to Biblical Doctrine*, 1994 p.1049).

3.0 The Word is Prophecy

Him. And when He spoke to me, He established His supremacy in my heart with the Words and answers He gave me. The two assertions derived from the four Biblical texts mentioned earlier (that is: (i) any viable discussion about the word of God must be Christ-centred and God-glorifying, and (ii) that every situation and inexplicable event in life must draw us back to God) confirmed His Words and answers to me about His sovereignty and forbearance over all personal prophesies. As I share with you that which the Lord revealed to me and which is central to *Prophecy*, I would like to quote some of those very words of revelation I shared in the sermon:

> I have been waiting on the Lord for some time now in respect of God's perfect will for my life. Some time after I presented the *A-Z Model of the Word* (that is my first published book) in this Fellowship (that is 'ced *The Way Fellowship – Hyde Park*') in October 1995, I was asked by the leader of the Fellowship *if I had a prophetic anointing because he was looking for people that will speak prophetically* to the Fellowship, and lay a new foundation. I went directly to the Father, not to any other source, for a clear meaning of *Prophecy*. On Wednesday 1 November, 1995 I had my breakthrough on the meaning of *Prophecy*. The Father responded: '*My Word; My Heart; Me; I Am; I Am Who I Am; Love; The Rabbi; Testimony; The Prophet of all Prophets; The source and channel of all information of all Godly Prophets; Jesus Christ is Prophecy; The Word is Prophecy*'.

I realised the identity of Him who spoke to me. The word of God from Genesis to Revelation recognises those identifications of His names, and these personifications of Him permeate the whole of the Scriptures. I swiftly realised the inter-relationships and equations between the different identifications and statements.

Take, for instance, the statement *The Word is Prophecy*, and let us discern the truth behind the statement. The statement can be separated into two key parts: (i) *The Word* and (ii) *Prophecy*. *The Word* will also mean God, Jesus Christ and the Holy Spirit (and also the Holy Scriptures from Genesis to Revelation). Therefore, in the statement *The Word is Prophecy*, the first part, *The Word*, can be replaced with any of the three persons of the Trinity and the Holy Bible. Then we can say any of the following: (i) *God is Prophecy*, (ii) *Jesus Christ is Prophecy*, (iii) *The Spirit of God is*

3.0 The Word is Prophecy

Prophecy and, (iv) *The Holy Bible is Prophecy*. What about the second part of the statement, *The Word is Prophecy* – that is *Prophecy*? Remember my earlier analogy and example on *Prophecy:* that Prophecy is God Himself personified, and every man created by God has different peculiarities. As every man is peculiar so are all personal prophecies. Therefore, if we can understand all the peculiarities in the 6 billion people of the world we must be close to understanding the fullness of God and all his prophecies! To know the depth of *Prophecy* (or the entire summation of all personal prophecies), we must therefore know the depth of God (the Trinity and the Holy Scriptures). Therefore, Prophecy is about God in three persons and the word of God. *The spectrum of Prophecy is God. The source of Prophecy is God.* Then we can input any of the following into the statement *The Word is Prophecy*: (i) *The Word is God*, (ii) *The Word is Jesus Christ*, (iii) *The Word is the Holy Spirit* and, (iv) *The Word is the Holy Bible*.

To simplify our example, the first part of the statement, *The Word is Prophecy* – that is, *The Word* – can be replaced to mean the following:

(i)   God is Prophecy
(ii) Jesus Christ is Prophecy
(iii) The Spirit of God is Prophecy
(iv) The Holy Bible is Prophecy.

The second part of the statement *The Word is Prophecy* – that is, *Prophecy* – can be replaced to mean the following:

(i)   *The Word is God*
(ii)   The Word is Jesus Christ
(iv) The Word is the Spirit of God
(v)   The Word is the Holy Bible.

Simultaneously, from the analogies of the two parts of the statement *The Word is Prophecy*, we can instantaneously say the following:

(i) *God is God*
(ii) *Jesus Christ is Jesus Christ*
(iii) *The Spirit of God is the Spirit of God*
(iv) *The Holy Bible is the Holy Bible (that is, the word of God from Genesis to Revelation is the word of God from Genesis to Revelation).*

Suffice to say, God is true and that He is specifically who He claims He is. Therefore, there is no other better definition for the word 'God' except the word God itself.

From the preceding stage, we can summarise each statement in one word:

(i) *God*
(ii) *Jesus Christ*
(iii) *Holy Spirit*
(iv) *The Word (that is, all the attributes, characteristics and functions that God personifies in the Holy Bible).*

It was this reasoning that provoked the publication of this book, *The Word is Prophecy*. In the first instance, the revelation of the names of God, and the discernment of the names through this exercise (*reason*) I consider awesome. The fact that any way we play with the subject matter *The Word is Prophecy*, we still get back to the revealed personalities of our Maker through this process is quite fascinating to me. For instance, *God is God*, we still got back to the revealed name and personality, God. From the preceding therefore we can also consider *The Word is Prophecy as the study of God as He has revealed Himself in many ways and the same way.*

Also from the derivation of God is God from *The Word is Prophecy*, we can deduce that a predominant way God has revealed Himself to us from the foregoing is that '*He is the Beginning and the End*'; '*The A–Z of Prophecies*'; '*The Alpha and Omega of all events*'. Therefore the notion, *That God is God, and His sovereignty remains in a dark world* is tenable and fulfils the two assertions of the four Bible texts: (i) that any viable discussion about the word of God must be Christ-centred and God-glorifying, and (ii) that every situation and inexplicable event in life must draw us back to God because only He has the secret answers to all things and mysteries. '*He is the Beginning and the End*'; '*The A–Z of Personal Prophecies*'; '*The Alpha and Omega of all events*'. Suffice to say, *God is the Lord of Prophecy* (that is, He is not ignorant of events and His presence is never far off. He is the God of encouragement and restoration!)

I would hereby like to take you back a little by answering the initial question which prompted this sermon and book, which is in two parts, asking: (i) *if I had a prophetic anointing* and (ii) *if I could speak prophetically* to the Fellowship. With the revelation of what *Prophecy in the broader context* meant, asking if I had a prophetic anointing and could speak to the Fellowship meant, in the first instance, *if I had God's anointing*; and, in the second instance, *if I can receive words from God* on behalf of the Fellowship respectively. To speak God's words will mean to possess God's anointing given by His grace. To possess God's anointing is to have a personal relationship with God and rest in Him and no other contrary power. To rest in God and to genuinely have God's anointing begins by knowing God and having a personal revelation of His sovereignty. I believe I know who He says He is, and the revelation of His presence is an ongoing process in my life. I continue to crave for more of His presence. Primarily, access to God's anointing means knowing the Father, the Son and the Holy Spirit (through the Word of God that is the Holy Scriptures from Genesis to Revelation), and to speak prophetically (or to prophesy) is a gift that derives from the knowledge of the first. How much of God's anointing we possess to hear and speak prophetically (that is ability to prophesy or personal prophetic anointing to discern and reveal events to others) will depend on the strength of the prophetic gift God has imparted upon us by His grace.

I have therefore answered in two parts the two part question and request, if I had prophetic anointing and could speak prophetically. To have prophetic anointing will mean (i) to have access to God's anointing (which is revealed in the knowledge of God the Father; God the Son and God the Holy Spirit, and the

3.0 The Word is Prophecy

word of God that is the Holy Bible), and to speak prophetically will mean (ii) to possess the gift of personal prophecy by His grace. (ii) is given as a result of (i). Therefore, the gift of personal prophecy must be subject to God's anointing, and not otherwise.

Prophecy is also about knowing the heart of God revealed through His Son, Jesus Christ. As God is sovereign, the person of Jesus Christ is central to understanding Prophecy in *'The Word is Prophecy'*. This line of thought becomes easier to understand as the person of Jesus Christ is illustrated in *The Prophecy Box* (see page 48). *The Prophecy Box* presents the analogy of the Trinity in the following way: the square-box represents God the Father, the circle represents Jesus Christ, and the Holy Spirit permeates all areas of the box. The co-existence of God in three persons is inseparable. *The Prophecy Box* is a definitive model on *Prophecy*. The model states that at the centre of the Father's throne (which is akin to His heart) is His Son (Rev. 7: 16–17). Jesus Christ is therefore a reflection of His father. Jesus Christ came to earth to take the place of the Father, and He is the light that must shine through the dark world of sin (1 John 4: 1–2). His light cannot be put off on earth. The person of Christ sustains the universe, and, as revealed in the box, His presence may be denied and not accepted by men but He cannot be hidden from. He sees all. Also as illustrated in *The Prophecy Box*, Jesus Christ's earthly presence in flesh and purpose hold firm the physical realm. An in depth study of *The Prophecy Box* will further broaden our understanding of God and *Prophecy*: that is, God equals the Trinity equals Prophecy ($G = T = P$). God's sovereignty is also revealed to be supreme in the make-up of the universe, and in all faculties of knowledge and existence[1].

As the centrality of Jesus Christ is established on earth, amongst other attributes revealed of Himself, He is acknowledged as the Lord Almighty of the Prophets. The Prophets of old received from Him and He was also addressed as one. Since the principal domain of the written word of God is in the physical realm and the centrality of Jesus Christ is established on earth, every discussion from Genesis to Revelation must begin with

---

[1] The facts revealed here about *The Prophecy Box* support other illustrations and descriptions that are given from time to time about the model in this book.

3.0 The Word is Prophecy

Jesus Christ and end with Jesus Christ. On a broader spectrum, every discussion of the Word must begin with the Word and end with the Word (John 1: 1–5). The truth of *Prophecy* is also about seeing the light of Christ: the Lord's truth personified in our vision, dreams and thoughts.

God is good, and is God. Is it really true? It is true most of us were brought up with our minds from childhood cultivated and trained to believe that God is good and not bad. In as much as man has striven to better his quality of life over the centuries, watching or reading any of the local and international television news and newspapers respectively, the gory nature and inexplicable mysteries of life began to reveal themselves all over the world. To the physical mind and the natural man, this truth about the dark world we live in is antithetical to all I have said about the positive nature of *Prophecy* and *personal prophecies*, and sovereignty of God over the universe and the world. God cannot be good and the world bad. God cannot be supreme and evil continue to reign in society. If *Prophecy* is indeed God-personified, personal prophecies are meant to encourage and not destroy. But it is indeed true we do receive negative personal prophecies (that is *reductive prophecies*). That was the state of my mind until God began to give specific answers concerning my worries.

As God revealed Himself (for instance, by saying *I Am, The Word, The Word is Prophecy*...) and despite the simplicity of His presence, my personal state of mind could not comprehend the extent of His goodness, neither was I able to separate the supremacy of His words from the evil of society. If *Prophecy* is indeed God personified and personal prophecies are meant to encourage, comfort and guide (that is positive word of encouragement and signs that portray God in good light), why all the evil of society and reductive prophecies (that is visions, dreams, occurrences and mysteries that cause pain and grief to us that are sometimes unpreventable)? This was my response to the Lord.

In fact, to be certain if indeed it was God that was speaking to me, I began to ask Him about the human life of struggles (also of pain, scheming and grief) in which we live. I asked, why do you reveal and release personal prophecies and visions that worry your children, Israel, and reduce us (for instance, cause grief, humiliation and bitterness)? For you said our life on earth is for a while. Why personal prophecies we cannot deal with? He said, I reduce you so that you may die to self and allow me to order your steps. I reduce you so that you may gain life, knowledge and understanding of me. I reduce you so that you will get closer and draw nearer to me. I reduce you so that you may be born-again and change your old ways. I reduce you so that you may be elevated, restored and have a vision and purpose in Christ Jesus. I reduce you so that you may fulfil destiny and the perfect will for your life. You see, without a vision and the revelation of Jesus Christ for your life, you cannot live a full life (or fulfil destiny). At times of reduction you draw nearer to me and seek me because you are helpless.

Again, it was only logical to me that because of sin and the very fact that our will is not very often synonymous with God's Will for our life, that is why we have reductive prophecies. It is therefore paramount that man's will equals God's Will ($w = W$) for *positive prophecies* to obtain. This is a condition whereby we become dead to self, and the dead works of Satan in our lives become un-operational. Therefore, the combination of both *positive-prophecies* and *reductive-prophecies* are the realities of our Christian life, even though we are born-again (that is, have accepted Jesus Christ and His authority into our personal lives). For we live in a world of sin, and reductive-prophecies will remain operational until we have the new heavens and the new earth when Matthew 6: 10 becomes operational ('your Kingdom come, your Will be done on earth as it is in heaven').

Indeed, the life of mankind today is not actually different from the historical facts, ways of life and life-pattern revealed about Biblical people of Israel, the children of God and the entire mankind in the word of God from Genesis to Revelation. Since Adam and Eve's sin (Genesis 3), man has been introduced to plurality of events. As the writer of the book of Ecclesiastes noted in Eccl. 3: 1–8,

> There is a time for everything, and a season for every activity under heaven: a time to be born and a time to die, a time to plant and a time to uproot, a time to kill and a time to heal, a time to

3.0 The Word is Prophecy

tear down and a time to build, a time to weep and a time to laugh, a time to mourn and a time to dance, a time to scatter stones and a time to gather them, a time to embrace and a time to refrain, a time to search and a time to give up, a time to keep and a time to throwaway, a time to tear and a time to mend, a time to be silent and a time to speak, a time to love and a time to hate, a time for war and a time for peace.

In this dark world, in its present state of sin and plurality, we are like wanderers still looking for a perfect place of rest and peace. In this world our perfect place of peace is in the fullness of Christ in our soul. Our perfect place of rest is eternal and is in heaven. For this world and our physical bodies are temporal and will pass away. But our soul will either go to hell or heaven; depending on whose side we are on, Satan's or Christ's respectively.

As the Spirit continued to speak, and I continued to discern what He was saying about our lives, He took me through some of His processes and footprints in our lives[1]. He showed me His character and personality in His word from Genesis to Revelation. For instance, despite all the struggles of *Israel* in the word of God, and all struggles that *Israel* may go through in the real world today, God's essence is for us to overcome Satan and evil in all situations. Once we are under Christ's refuge and His Spirit dwells in us, His ultimate plan is to restore *Israel* and His children to Himself, and only to Himself, for His glorification. His purpose and ultimate objective is to restore us to our perfect and rightful position at creation before the inception of sin, reincarnated children washed by the blood of the lamb. The Lord said, *'every situation must bring Israel back to me'*. And I reasoned: that is why when a new child is born we gather before God and thank Him, and when loved ones die we still gather to Him for comfort, strength and to thank Him for a life well spent. Every situation will bring *Israel* and the children of God back to Him. The Lord is with *Israel* and surrounds *Israel* all the time, and both in life and in death because we return to Him. This reasoning to me was awesome. And I cried: 'Alleluyah! Alleluyah Father! The Lord is

---

[1] This I have elaborated and used in describing *The Prophecy Box* in many ways throughout this book.

with *Israel* – all the time! Abba Father, Immanuel God with us!'

All situations must bring us to God. Looking back now, I remember my late grandmother, Emmanuella Ogunmuyiwa on her deathbed, slowly emaciating and dying of arthritis, and how her death pains, particularly in the years 1989 and 1990, drew me closer to God. Looking back now, I remember in January 1990 humbling myself before God, praying fervently and asking Him to ease her pain. Although I had a Christian upbringing living with Grandma, and I loved her endearing and upright Christian personality, I would not claim I had a full understanding and realisation of what my personal responsibilities as a Christian were to God, and what making a personal commitment to serve and worship Him fully meant. Although I carried her handbag from one Church to another whilst I was a young child, it was in this period of her dying and subsequent death that I was praying incessantly, that I went through a new Christian rebirth (that is the born-again experience of making personal commitment to Jesus Christ as my Lord and Saviour). I just wanted to know, serve and worship God. I had to open up my spirit and for God to fill me. The process was slow because I detested any form of 'fundamentalism' that was associated with all forms of religion. It was not too long before I committed my ways to the path of Christ in Sokoto, Nigeria in January 1990 and confessed the faith publicly in Bauchi State, Nigeria in August 1990. *It is a fact of life that when we are alone, weary and helpless, and there seems to be no meaning to life, we seek for what we do not know. And that which we do not know is God. Our plight brings us back to God. To Him we consciously or unconsciously believe has the answers. Invariably, whether we are Christian-believers or not, that inexplicable factor that is God who has perfect understanding of all inexplicable mysteries cannot be removed from existence.*

God lords over our existence, and we cannot take Him away from existence. As we continue to observe the demise of Christian ethics and morality in society, I remember in 1995 it is a shame that it took the unfortunate and unjustifiable deaths of the sixteen children in a primary school at Dunblane in Scotland for the spirit of the nation and her people to be moved in a way we had never seen before in the United Kingdom, and the same

3.0 The Word is Prophecy

happened in the United States post September 11, 2001, to begin to seek answers to these inexplicable mysteries and state of moral decadence of the nation. The week following the killings (particularly the Sunday following the killings) almost everyone was in church, asking, why? Again, as I mentioned earlier, *it is a fact of life that when we are alone, weary and helpless, and there seems to be no meaning to life, we seek for what we do not know. And that which we do not know is God. Our plight brings us back to God. To Him who we consciously or unconsciously believe has the answers. Invariably, whether we are Christian-believers or not, that inexplicable factor to life that is God, who has perfect understanding of all inexplicable mysteries, cannot be removed from existence whether we love him or not.* When ungodliness persists, the devil has his way. Reduction is the work of Satan. I continue to tell those around me that we cannot disassociate the prosperity of the United Kingdom from when she knew God and righteousness reigned in the land[1]. Looking at the beauty and density of the church-buildings in the land, and how much God was planted in the statutes of the land, one cannot but be amazed that this was once a nation of people that knew the majesty and experienced the glory of God. The United Kingdom must be won for Jesus Christ again and righteousness must reign in the land. As a trained economist I know that the answers to this nation's problems are not in the hands of the economists or the politicians, but solely in the hand of God. I particularly see those Africans (particularly Nigerians) that came into the UK to settle in the 1980s and early 1990s first as witnesses for Jesus Christ. I have heard this said in Christian conferences, and I have also primarily come to the personal conclusion that we are not primarily here for economic and educational reasons amongst many other reasons. Many were already committed Christians in Nigerian universities and higher institutions, and not many will say they

---

[1] Although personally I have had another contending argument in a theological setting (presumably by an English lady at Oxford) that at the same period the country was a leading slave trader and imperialist. Maybe I must have sounded too apologetic during the discussion. But in fact it is possible to theologically investigate and correlate the former prosperity of the UK to her relationship with God. It is a fact that the word of God is absolute but the appreciation of that truth revealed in the word is progressive amongst men. Hence the dilemma of Great Britain at the time.

ever contemplated living in the UK for a long time whilst growing up in Nigeria! I believe it is also true of those Nigerians in the USA and other western nations where Christian norms are quickly being discarded and actually being dumped into the rubbish bin! But Jesus Christ is alive!

It is therefore paramount that we accept the sovereignty of God, and Jesus Christ the centre of His truth. When we know God, *reduction* will lead to *restoration*, and evil will lead to good. Ungodliness will lead to godliness. Accepting Jesus Christ and not letting go of Him in crises will lead to *restoration* for Israel, Christians and the nation. It releases *positive prophecies* and good works. *Positive prophecies* lead to *testimonies*, and *testimonies is about how we have overcome evil obstacles of Satan. How they have overcome (and continue to overcome) is the story of Israel and the descendants of Israel.* Look at the stories of those who lived by faith: Abraham, Moses, Joseph, Daniel, David and all those mentioned in Hebrew 11 (the Bible roll of honour) and many more today. It is about how they overcame by the blood of the lamb and the power of God. Look at those barren women that later gave birth to children, and the healing of the sick, blind and the miracles of Jesus Christ. *As testimony is the story of the fathers of faith, so is testimony the essence of faith. Testimony is God-personified.*

As I continued to hear God, He said, I am *the Lord of Prophecies* (that is positive prophecy of encouragement and restoration); so far you are in me and I am in you. *Prophecy* is about *Testimony*. *Testimony* is about the prophetic word of God saying the final authority of the heavens and the earth are mine. And that Christian-believers own the world. His word will come to pass. He is a God who never fails. He makes the impossible possible. He reveals the end from the beginning. The Lord never forgets His own. As Psalm 137: 5–6 says, 'If I forget you, O Jerusalem, may my right hand forget its skill May my tongue cling to the roof of my mouth if I do not remember you, if I do not consider Jerusalem my highest joy '. He is a God of testimonies – a God that fulfils all promises and meets the needs of all. He has never failed.

As gruesome as the sufferings of the Jews were in the Second World War, the creation of the modern nation of Israel in 1948 was an aftermath of those sufferings. *Restoration* came after *reduction* by the Nazis. Concerning the nightmare of pain, wars and disaster all over the world there will be restoration in due season. God reigns.

4.0 Prophecy

In this book, *Prophecy* is categorized into two types. The two types of Prophecy are: (i) *Prophecy (or Prophecy in the broader context)* and (ii) *personal prophecy*.

Prophecy (or Prophecy in the broader context), is defined as the word of God beginning from the book of Genesis to Revelation, inspired by the Holy Spirit, written by the fingers of God in the hearts of men. There is nothing new to add to the Holy Scriptures, and in the Holy Scriptures from Genesis to Revelation are various situations in life which may occur. *As every situation is subject to the Holy Scripture, and not otherwise, so is every personal prophecy subject to Prophecy.*

Personal prophecy is defined as message for men for strengthening, encouragement and comfort (1 Cor. 14: 3) and for edification of the Church (1 Cor. 14: 4). The *means of personal prophecy* are: (i) Oral report through men (*vessels*) outside of Scriptures. Men are hereby considered as *vessels of prophecy*; (ii) vision and; (iii) direction through dreams. But *personal prophecy* is not our specific study in this book. The intention of this book is to exposit a global understanding of *Prophecy in the broader context* so as to be able to have better understanding of *personal prophecies* as it relates to us individually and the Church. It is believed much has not been done in this respect.

As our intention is primarily on *Prophecy in the broader context*, we therefore focus more on the word (the Holy Scriptures and the patterns, concepts, events of life and living-patterns exposited in it) and the Word of God (Jesus Christ). Jesus Christ the Son of God lived an exemplary life. His existence in flesh, sufferings and eventual death are proof that every situation and test that may occur to man are no longer new, and that He served as a living sacrifice for all creation. The written word of God (the Holy Scriptures) and the living Word of God Jesus Christ) are one and are *Prophecy*. Jesus Christ's detractors knew and called Him

4.0 Prophecy

Prophecy! (Mark 14: 65). Jesus Christ identified with the Old Testament writings about Himself (Matt. 5: 17–19; Luke 24: 27; John 5: 39, 4: 0). As the Old and the New Testaments are one continuous story of Jesus Christ (*The Word*), so are they also a continuous story of *Prophecy*. Suffice to say, *The Word is Prophecy*.

Although in this present world we have a duality of *personal prophecy* and *Prophecy in the broader context* which will continue until Jesus Christ comes back, the word of God (the Holy Scriptures) is perfect, and *Prophecy in the broader context* is perfect. The written word from Genesis to Revelation, that is that which exists in the physical realm and is given to us by the Holy Spirit is perfect. Although, in this life in its present form *personal prophecy* has not ceased and can be imperfect. Imperfection of *personal prophecy* will continue until Jesus Christ comes back. When Jesus Christ comes, interpretation of the word of God (the Holy Scriptures) will no longer be difficult because there will no longer be need for exposition of the Word; and also there will no longer be division of opinion amongst churches and denominations about the Word. Therefore, *personal prophecy* will cease and perfection only will reign (that is *Prophecy* or *Prophecy in the broader context*) due to the coming of our Lord Jesus Christ. Then there will no longer be duality of *personal prophecy* and *Prophecy in the broader context* as it obtains now in the present world.

Hence, there are two stages of *perfection of prophecy* (or *perfect prophecy*), which I have identified:

(i) Stage 1 is about this present world whereby the perfection which obtains rests solely in the word of God (that is the Holy Scriptures) which is with us in the physical realm. The perfection which mankind is asked to attain by God is revealed solely in the word of God. *Personal prophecy* still exists and is meant to be subject to the word of God.

(ii) Stage 2 is about when Jesus Christ (*The Word*) Himself returns. The absolute nature of His presence in the world will make *personal prophecy* cease. Then there will be no form of imperfection and all forms of error in the Church will cease. *Prophecy* (that is *Prophecy in the broader context*) will only remain, and 1 Cor. 13: 8–13 will be true.

1 Corinthians 13: 8–13 reveals 'Love never fails. But where there are prophecies (*that is personal prophecy, I insert*), they will cease; where there are tongues, they will be stilled; where there is knowledge, it will pass away. For we know in part and we prophecy in part (*that is personal prophecies are revealed in part, I exposit*), but when perfection (*that is Jesus Christ/The Word/ Prophecy/The Word is Prophecy, I add*) comes, the imperfect (*personal prophecy, I insert*) disappears. When I was a child, I talked like a child, I thought like a child, I reasoned like a child (*an analogy on state of imperfection/immaturity of personal prophecy, I insert*). When I became a man I put childish ways behind me (*assumed state of imperfection/maturity, I insert*). Now we see but a poor reflection as in a mirror (*still state of imperfection and non-100% accurate of personal prophecy in the present world, I induct*); then we shall see face to face (*state of perfection of prophecy, when Christ comes, I add*). Now I know in part (*state of imperfection*); then I shall know fully, even as I am fully known (*state of perfection of prophecy, I insert*). And now these three remain: faith, hope and love.' The supremacy of Love is extolled in *The Prophecy Box*.

5.0 The Prophecy Box

A model of *Prophecy* (or a pictorial illustration of *Prophecy*) has been developed which I call *The Prophecy Box* (another rod and an offshoot of the *A–Z Model of the Word*). *The Prophecy Box* is very simple to understand if studied methodically. *The Prophecy Box* is also a unique Analogy of the Trinity: The square box represents

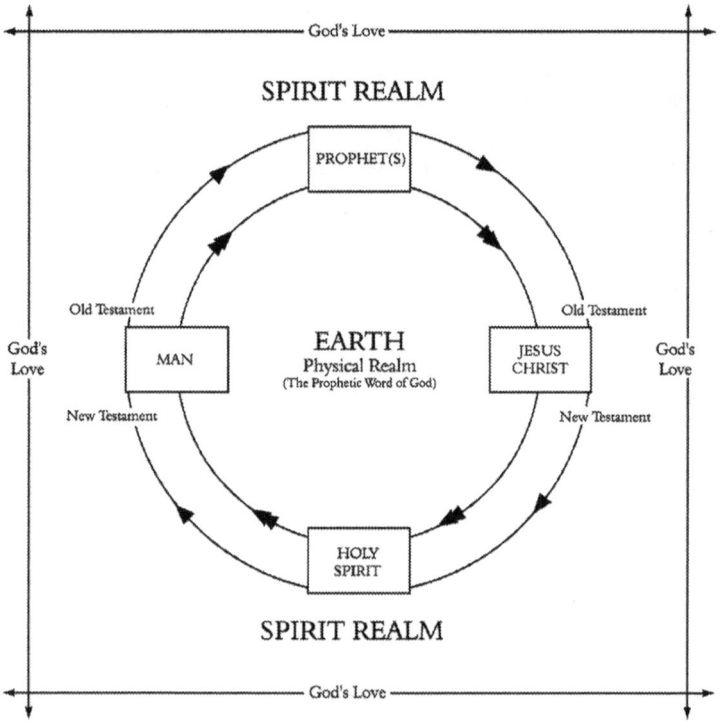

5.0 The Prophecy Box

God the Father; the larger of the two circles represents Jesus Christ the Son; and the Holy Spirit (that is the spirit of Jesus Christ) permeates every area and four corners of the entire box[1].

---

[1] This Analogy of the Trinity is also true for the A–Z Model of the Word. For those who have read the A–Z Model of the Word (first printed, December 1995) or will do hereafter should replace the Holy Spirit in the inner circle or centre of the box on page 8 of the book with Jesus Christ. And just as in *The Prophecy Box*, the Holy Spirit also permeates all areas and four corners of the entire box of the A–Z Model of the Word. Thus the Analogy of the Trinity in both The Prophecy Box and the A–Z Model of the Word are one and the same.

The Prophecy Box is an inspirational work of the Holy Spirit, but as I continue to use this *Analogy of the Trinity* (that is the box) for different writings I have discovered and had to accept that my knowledge of economic thought and theory, particularly the work of Werner Hildenbrand, *Core and Equilibria of a large economy,* (Princeton University Press, 1974 p.123), has also been an influence in my constructive and logical pattern of thought and dissertation in my theological writings. However, in no way are they exact replica nor do they deal with the same issues. In fact, Hildenbrand used the expression of the *core* (that is the centre) on how market prices are set, and how a large economy moves to the centre in analysing the Edgeworth Box (1881) and Walras. Applying this pattern of thought to Christian theology, Jesus Christ being at the centre of *The Prophecy Box* reflects the entire character of God, which embodies the entire box. Knowing that Jesus Christ is an exact reflection of God and the power of the Holy Spirit which permeates the entire area of *The Prophecy Box* continually changes the personality of the Christian-believer so as to resemble the exact personality of Christ at the centre. The analogy of the Trinity states that as we receive more of God's love and presence of the Holy Spirit, we become like Jesus Christ at the centre of the model. That is, the entire box moves towards the core of *The Prophecy Box*. Christ the only begotten Son of God is a child born out of His father's love (John 3: 16). And just as the human body, whereby the human conception and pregnancy is carried in the centre of the body, Christ is at the centre of God and His central theme.

This uniqueness of the concept of the centre I have had to use in explaining *the development of economies and societies in relation to their central government, leadership, and other institutions of society. For example, I will say a leader of a church, community, society or country is an exact reflection of the various people representing such institutions, particularly when such a leader is not imposed from outside.* As simple as this may seem, it has given me much peace and better understanding of development and developing economies in recent times. However, I have gone through different stages of thought before arriving at this conclusion. My forthcoming publication on *Faith and Reason* reflects this understanding of institutions, economies and societies.

5.1 DESCRIPTION OF THE MODEL

Since the word of God (the Holy Bible) is an integrated whole, *The Prophecy Box* chronicles various patterns and concepts therein. The various patterns and concepts identified within the Holy Bible are uniquely designed to fit into the box, and there is still possibility for further improvement and development of the various ideas.

God is Prophecy. The spirit of God is the spirit of Prophecy. The infinite personality and size of God is mirrored in the box. The Prophecy Box proves the omniscient qualities of God – as one having infinite knowledge and understanding of the universe and every form of existence of which He happens to be the author. The boundaries of the box are infinitely determined, since God is Love and the length, breadth, width and height of God's Love cannot be measured nor fathomed. The objective of the analysis of the box is to demonstrate that Prophecy is about the word of God (from Genesis to Revelation), and the Word (that is God the Father, God the Son and God the Holy Spirit) is Prophecy. The box mirrors the possible/ revealed extremes and extent of Prophecy – height, length, breadth and width of Prophecy.

The various patterns and concepts are:

5.1 (i) God's Love

God is Love (1 John 4: 16). *The Prophecy Box* is bounded by God's other revealed name, *Love*. The extent of the height, breadth, length and width of God's Love we cannot grasp and estimate (Ephesians 3: 18). *The Prophecy Box* is square-shaped with infinite expanse at every height, length, breadth and width, and that is why each line is with a spear-shaped arrow that points towards a specific direction without limits. The expanse of God's Love is beyond our understanding and unfathomable.

Therefore, the square-shaped box represents God. In the middle of the square-shaped box are two circles. The outer circle represents Jesus Christ. Jesus Christ the Son is at the core of the Father's heart (Rev. 7: 17). In the heart of God the Father is His

Son. Jesus is the heart of the Father – His conscience, light and truth. That is why His truth must shine throughout the universe. All Christians have the mandate to spread the Gospel, and we know it. We cannot take Jesus Christ away from creation or from life and existence. And that is why those who do not know or accept Him are said to be condemned. That was why He left us with a message of salvation to be ministered in all the earth and in every corner of the world. That was why He trained, and sent before Him His Apostles and the seventy-two, in twos and threes, and not just one to go into the villages and towns in His lifetime to spread the Gospel. He taught them how to do that. And His Spirit is still here with us. Just as the wind permeates the whole of the earth, so does the Holy Spirit permeate all the universe (both the heavens and the earth, and the spirit and physical realms respectively).

As we receive more of God's Love by conforming to God's holy standards, we become more like Jesus Christ and draw the heavens closer to earth as Jesus Christ requested in Matthew 6: 10. Matthew 6: 10 says 'your kingdom come, your will be done on earth as it is in heaven'.

God is Love. His Love He exalts above every other thing. King David in Psalm 138: 2 noted '…for your love and your faithfulness, for you have exalted above all things your name and your word'.

5.1 (ii) *The Word, or any of the names associated with God in three persons (God the Father, God the Son and God the Holy Spirit)*

Any of the names associated with God, Jesus Christ and the Holy Spirit will fit into *The Prophecy Box*. And how each name specifically fits into the box can be elaborately explained, but it is beyond the scope of this study, although an illustration and example will be given.

Some of the names associated with God and Jesus Christ are Love, Ancient of Days, The Messiah, The Only Begotten of God, The Alpha and Omega, The Word and the Sword of the Spirit, Bright Morning Star; Author of life, Mighty God, Incarnate Son, Mighty Son of God, Logos, The Holy Spirit, Chief Cornerstone, Man of Sorrows, Holy and

5.0 The Prophecy Box

Anointed, Everlasting Father, Light of the World, Righteous Judge, Prince of Peace, the Great High Priest, Water of Life, Lamb of God, King of Glory, King of Heaven, The Great I Am, King of Kings, Immanuel, Resurrection and life, Son of Righteousness, The Galilean, The Good Shepherd, The Nazarene, Jesus of Nazareth, First Born, Strength and Song, Lord of Hosts, Lord of Glory, Son of Man, The Lord's Anointed, The lion of Judah, Rod of Jesse, Son of David, Deliverer, Author and Finisher of Faith, Author of life, Word Made Flesh, The Anointed One, Prophecy! Etc.[1]

As an illustration, we can fit the terminology *Ancient of Days* into *The Prophecy Box*. Our creator is called *Ancient of Days* and associated with ancient paths (Jeremiah 6: 16–19). For example, His creation such as the heavens and earth are ancient in history and His authority and power predates the creation of man and His covenant with Biblical people of Israel. The creation of the heavens and the earth splits *The Prophecy Box* into two parts – the spirit realm and the physical realm. Man lives in the physical realm and the history of the world predates four thousand years of recorded history since Noah. That I consider ancient, and fits perfectly into the pictorial illustration of *Prophecy* (p.32).

Some of the names, qualities and roles associated with the Holy Spirit are Wonderful Counsellor, The Truth, Older Brother, Advocate, Guide, Instructor, Ever Refreshing, Refiller, Nourisher, Refuge, Protector, Trainer, Honour, Consecrator, Sanctifier, Transformer, Builder, Enabler, Leader, Companion, Quickener, Supplier of all Needs, Supporter, Sustainer.

For example, we can also fit the name *Holy Spirit* into the box. Just as we cannot see the wind and it permeates the whole of the earth, so does the Holy Spirit permeate all the universe (both the heavens and the earth, and the spirit and physical realms respectively). The *Holy Spirit* is the power and the Lord's zeal to affect His own authority and commandments. At the same speed at which God Almighty spoke at the beginning of creation, His power and zeal (that is the *Holy Spirit*) created the heavens and the earth (Genesis 1: 1). The *Holy Spirit made the unseen seen.*

---

[1] All these names of God and Jesus Christ are in various parts of the Holy Bible.

5.1 (iii) Genesis to Revelation (i.e. word of God/the Holy Bible)

The Prophecy Box covers all the Christian's experience in life from Genesis to Revelation, and the genealogy of creation to the close of the age and the second coming of Jesus Christ.

5.1 (iv) The Theory of Prophecy.

The Prophecy Box describes in abstract terms who God says He is and the realities of man's existence. Christ being at the centre of *The Prophecy Box* is a reflection of His father. Creation from the genealogy of man to the close of the age are products of *Prophecy*. In respect of realities of man's existence, two specific methods of God in dealing with man permeate the word of God from the book of Genesis to Revelation: they are the methods *of visualisation to realisation and reduction to restoration*. Visualisation (that is divine perception), reduction and restoration are also the realities of Christian living. In reality, the world also physically witnessed the sufferings of Jesus Christ.

5.1 (v) The Spirit Realm and the Physical Realm.

The Prophecy Box also describes the activities of the realms of the spirit and the physical. In the spirit realm we receive visions and dreams. In the physical realm, we have the written word of God, the Holy Bible and the information of the Prophets. The ministration of the Holy Spirit encompasses both the spirit and the physical realms; thus the power of the Holy Spirit permeates both the spiritual and physical life of every Christian.

To what extent do Christians enjoy the effective power and anointing of the Holy Spirit? This will depend on how much we conform to the holy standards of God, and this specific question is answered in the section where we deal with *How to deal with reductive prophecies*.

5.1 (vi) The Heavens and the Earth

The Prophecy Box describes the heavens and the earth. The swiftness of God in creating the heavens and the earth proves His omnipotence – His unlimited power. In the spirit realm we have

5.0 The Prophecy Box

the heavens and in the physical realm we have the earth. The domain and reign of the Almighty God encompasses both the heavens and the earth because He created both. In the summer months of 1995, Jeremiah 10: 12 and Psalm 8 fascinated me so much every time I read them and they both refer to the heavens and the earth. In fact to *experience how majestic God was* – Psalm 8: 1 – was my prayer request in those summer months. And I thank God for His personal revelation of Himself in my life. He is majestic and above all circumstances and situations.

Psalm 8 says 'O Lord, our Lord, how majestic is your name in all the earth! You have set your glory above the heavens. From the lips of children and infants you have ordained praise because of your enemies, to silence the foe and the avenger. When I consider your heavens, the work of your fingers, the moon and the stars, which you have set in place, what is man that you are mindful of him, the son of man that you care for him? You made him a little lower than the heavenly beings and crowned him with glory and honour. You made him ruler over the works of your hands; you put everything under his feet: all flocks and herds, and the beasts of the field, the birds of the air, and the fish of the sea, all that swim the paths of the seas. O Lord, our Lord, how majestic is your name in all the earth!'

Jeremiah 10: 12 says 'But God made the earth by his power; He founded the world by his wisdom and stretched out the heavens by his understanding. When he thunders, the waters in the heavens roar; he makes clouds rise from the ends of the earth. He sends lightning with the rain and brings out the wind from his storehouses.'

The clear revelation that God and the authority of God are present everywhere, and the foundations of both heavenly and earthly existence were laid by Him, and only His power sustains the universe, I consider awesome and true. *In essence, The Prophecy Box also describes the sustenance of the universe (and/or the firmaments).*

5.1 (vii) The Preparation Model

The Prophecy Box describes how God ultimately prepares His children for reigning with Him. Both the inner and outer circles in the box describe *the preparation pattern of God* of dealing with His

5.0 The Prophecy Box

people. God always had good ideas and vision for Israel and the world.

Man is inherently sinful. At every stage of Israel's life God continued to prepare them through the Judges and the Prophets He sent despite Israel's sin in His presence. They worshipped foreign and other gods. The Prophets were different in personality but had a common approach in addressing the sin of Israel. God prepared them for their call to bring the people back to Him, even when the people never knew they were doing wrong before God. First, the Prophets rebuked the people and then they cried out for atonement before the Lord. With renewal in the spirit of *Israel* to rededicate themselves to the Lord came redemption of sin, promise of salvation and restoration and deliverance by God and also praise and thanksgiving by Israel. This was the pattern set by God for the Judges and the Prophets in the Old Testament. In the New Testament, this pattern of preparation for the salvation of our Lord was also followed by John the Baptist, who prepared the way for Jesus Christ. Jesus Christ also followed this pattern of crying to the people for atonement and promise of salvation. Before Jesus Christ left, He prepared the Apostles and the Seventy-two to go before Him into the villages and towns with the same mandate. He adequately prepared them for their new roles, since He knew He would be leaving soon. He was rejected and killed like His old Prophets. He left the Holy Spirit with His own (His Disciples and Apostles), to counsel them and to continue this same old *pattern of hope and atonement*, and bringing all back to Him. And He promised that He will wash all anew like new born babies and His Spirit shall dwell in those that turn away from their old ways of sinful living.

That is why those who believe in this *preparation model* and do convert to the new kingdom are called *born-again* Christians. All Christians have the ultimate call to go into all corners of the world and bring all men to God and to prepare them for their salvation until the day of Jesus Christ when He shall come again in flesh and establish His kingdom on earth. Evil will have finally receded and the light of Christ will then be able to brighten the earth in its fullest glow. Then there will be no more sin and we shall be perfect people dead to our Adamic and evil selves once and for all and now in the image of God (real men fully keyed into the Spirit of Life) as He created us in the beginning. And there shall be no conflict amongst one another and no pain. And there will be new heavens and earth where all will live in peace.

There are typical examples in the *preparation model* that permeates the word of God from Genesis to Revelation. Throughout in the word of God, God always prepared the highway for a major event (i.e. through His prophets, judges and other means). For instance, Noah prepared the way for peace between God and His new creation for the best of God to take place (Genesis 8); the Prophets (i.e. Isaiah) and John the Baptist prepared the way for Christ; the seventy-two prepared the way for Christ before He entered every village and town; Jesus prepared His apostles before He left the world, and gave the Holy Spirit, the Counsellor; the outpouring of God's anointing (as on the day of Pentecost [Acts 2: 1–13]) on all who confess that 'Jesus is Lord' (i.e. believers), and the availability of that power that existed at creation made available that we may become a new creation in the perfect image of God the way we were before the sin of Adam and Eve.

Prophecy prepares the way for God's blessings. Many situations, events and people will prepare the way for God's perfect will for our lives. To key into God's blessings may mean many rivers to cross. The prophetic word prepares the way for God's perfect blessings in our lives.

5.1 (viii) The Visualisation and Realisation Experience

The Prophecy Box also describes the two methods (*modus operandi*) of God, and the first is the *method of visualisation to realisation* by man in His earthly daily walk. Godly-vision and a sense of purpose and destiny separate men, churches, governments, leaders, institutions and nations from those who are not their kind.

Man created in God's image (Genesis 1: 26–27) is so blessed and given a visionary spirit, talents and the willpower to accomplish Godly defined purposes on earth. It is important and a challenge for every man to discover those talents and unique gifts planted within him, and vision that would release him into his perfect destiny. Godly vision and a sense of purpose will give full satisfaction in life. Man is created in the image of God and God took of what was within Himself, invisible with the naked eye, and created (or realised) the visible universe. The discovery or lack of this vision and perfect purpose in life makes the difference between success and failure and between hope and death and between perverse living and respect of other people. Discovery or lack of vision makes the difference between rich and poor nations, governments, churches, institutions and families. Discovery of a vision is like a springboard to other things, progress and breakthrough in locked-up areas to realisation (fulfilment of destiny or purpose). It was with the knowledge of the capability of the spiritual deposits within Himself (i.e. visionary spirit of creation and ability of realisation of creation) that God created the heavens and the earth. And this measure of visionary spirit and creative power, He had planted in us ever since the beginning of creation. At the same speed He spoke, He created the heavens and the earth. The Lord's faith and zeal in His Word created the heavens and the earth. He saw the vision (and conceived) how the heavens and the earth would look and He realised them. Like tiny seeds that grow to become a forest, vision grows to be realised. The process of growth may be difficult, and this issue of difficulty leads us to the second method of God, *The method of reduction to restoration*.

We can therefore liken *The Prophecy Box* to an invisible seed within God that did sprout to life and visibility, to become the heavens and the earth because God wanted it so. This is the method of visualisation to realisation experience.

5.1 (ix) The Reductive and Restoration Experience

This is the second *modus operandi* of God. Every great personality in the Bible experienced some form of reduction before they were *restored* and lifted up, including Jesus Christ Himself, Job, Isaiah, Daniel, Samson etc. They were all reduced to be lifted up by God. Their experiences prepared them for their future responsibilities and peculiar roles in life. In humiliation they also learnt forgiveness. Nelson Mandela of South Africa is a very good example.

A unique example was Jesus Christ – even in the face of death

5.0 The Prophecy Box

He still took one in His train to heaven (Luke 23: 43). Despite being reduced and humiliated in flesh by men, Jesus still blessed and took one of those hung on the cross with Him to paradise. On the third day of death He was lifted up and elevated to play a new role as wonderful Counsellor and Almighty God in the form of the Holy Spirit that dwells in Christian-believers (John 16: 7). The Holy Spirit takes from what is Jesus'. John 16: 14–15 says, 'He will bring glory to me by taking from what is mine and making it known to you. All that belongs to the Father is mine. That is why I said the Spirit will take from what is mine and make it known to you.'

Another personality in the 'Bible roll of honour' that went through *the reductive and restorative experience* was Joseph (Genesis 37–48). Joseph dreamt that his brothers were going to bow down to him and in the process he experienced humiliation for God's glory and promise to be ultimately revealed and accomplished. He was sold by his brothers to foreigners (the Ishmaelites) and ended up in the land of Egypt. He found favour in the household of Pharaoh's captain of the guard, Potiphar, and prospered. Potiphar, Pharaoh's wife, found him attractive and wanted to sleep with him. He fled and was accused of rape, and eventually ended up in the place where the king's prisoners were confined. But a talent of interpretation of dreams planted in him by the Father was quickened and made useful for his eventual release from prison and immediate elevation to a place of responsibility as the governor of Egypt, and only second to Pharaoh in the land. As Christ took some in His train to heaven so also Joseph learnt forgiveness when he met his brothers and also blessed his family by bringing seventy-five of them to share in his fortune in Egypt.

In Christ Jesus, to be reduced is to be lifted up.

5.1 (x) The Deep Theory

The Prophecy Box is also described as God's Love. *Prophecy* is deep (a mystery) and it is also about receiving of God's Love. Therefore a pre-knowledge of events is a gift born of God's Love. It takes a deep sense of spirituality to understand the extent of God's Love. At the core and centre of the box is Jesus Christ, and Christ is a child born of God's Love. To know the depth of God's Love is to know Jesus Christ. John 3: 16 says, 'For God so loved the world that He gave His only begotten Son that whoever believes in Him shall not perish but have eternal life'. That Jesus Christ had to die for my sins and your sins – the depth of that sacrifice and love we cannot fathom. And the knowledge that He rose again is deep (and also a mystery): the message of resurrection is deep. The deepness of God's Love for His Son is unfathomable and for us who believe in His Son. For God to reveal a future event to us or embark on spiritual gossip for our sake is a mystery. The depth of that love is not measurable and it is a mystery. To receive a *personal prophecy* from the Holy Spirit is to receive from the deep well of God and of His Son (i.e. of His love, knowledge, guidance, mercy, grace). To prophecy based on the Word of God is to experience the mystical and be close to Him (God the Father, God the Son and God the Holy spirit).

Again, *Prophecy* is deep and spirituality is all about seeing through the heart of God – Jesus Christ. In the heart of God is His Word – His promise of His Son and *restoration* that all the Prophets spoke about will come in flesh to the world. If you are in Christ Jesus and He is in you, a prophetic message in its worst decorum, however pictured in the mind, must eventually reveal God's glory and love for you on earth or when you get to heaven. For God is Love and merciful, and every *personal prophecy* and prophetic message must bring those who believe back to Him to receive of His love, mercy and grace through Christ Jesus. Although we sometimes panic and are worried, because some *personal prophecies* received do not seem to say good things about future events. But 1 John 4: 4 says, 'You, dear children, are from God and have overcome them, because the one who is in you is greater than the one who is in the world'. Revelation 12: 11 says, 'They overcame him by the blood of the Lamb and by the word of their testimony; they did not love their lives so much as to shrink from death'. For we are winners, victorious and successful in Christ Jesus on earth and in the heavens. That is what the word of God says about us and as we are spiritual beings we have to begin to study the word of God with spiritual eyes and not physical eyes, that we may believe and receive what the Word says. It is, therefore, important that we invite the Holy Spirit every time we read the spiritual word of God. Our spiritual eyes and hearts opened to receive of the word of God will cast out all fears and anxieties. For the light of Christ will shine through the dark clouds of our situations.

Prophecy is also about revelation of the deep and secret things of God. When Jesus Christ lived on earth, His truth, personality and what He encompassed were sometimes difficult to grasp. Jesus Christ, the truth of God, is spiritually deep, as the essence of the earth within the universe is deep to the natural mind. With the death of Jesus Christ, His ascension, and the gift of the Holy Spirit, His truth and essence became clearer not only to His disciples but also to His Believers.

Therefore, how do we grasp the mystery of God? First, we must believe that Jesus Christ is our Lord and Saviour, and also accept that the word of God is true and infallible. We must also adhere to the holy standards of God, for example, through fasting, prayer, meditation, praise and worship of His holy name. Becoming deep in the things of God is a gradual process. All in the Bible roll of honour had a deep sense of spirituality (Hebrew 11). The books in the Bible from Genesis to Revelation are deeply spiritual. You and I must continually make inquest into this mystery within *Prophecy*.

5.1 (xi) The Gospel Truth Model

We can also describe the box as *The Gospel Truth Model (GTM)* because the model describes the truth of the Gospel of Jesus Christ and the word of God, which is at the centre of the box. Jesus is the light of the world and the truth of the Gospel. Every good and bad situation in life and death must bring us back to Jesus Christ so far as we are in Him (and under His refuge) and not in the camp of the enemy (Satan). Jesus Christ as the light and the truth of the world gives understanding and is the reason why we exist. That is why when we give birth, or someone dies, in marriage and whatever situation, we gather to acknowledge Him believing that He is our creator-Immanuel, God with us.

The GTM says that as God's chosen children we are created with different talents, vision and purposes by God to fulfil destiny. We are God's witnesses of His mighty hand and that He is God – those He has chosen and created for His glory (Isaiah 43: 7–10). As peculiar individuals we are all on earth to fulfil a purpose to the glory of God. We are the children of Israel, His first love – a peculiar nation set apart for the Lord. It is the truth of God and the Christian's life that the gospel of King Jesus Christ must be preached to every corner of the world -His light must shine throughout our dark world. And until the light of Jesus Christ shines throughout the world we must give Satan no rest.

The word of God is prophetic and it is about the truth of Jesus Christ shining throughout the world. There shall be no *reductive prophecies* (for instance, storm, humiliation, destruction, disaster etc.) in a new world where there exists no sin and the light of Christ is perfectly shining in all corners.

5.1 (xii) *The Old and the New Testament are One and Continuous*

The truth of Jesus Christ in the New Testament books was prophetic – the prophets in the Old Testament spoke about it. Jesus also acknowledged, identified and believed the Old Testament writings (Matt 5: 17–19; Luke 24: 27; John 5: 39, 40). The preparation story sees Him (Jesus) as the bridge between the Old and the New Testament. All the various books in the Holy Scriptures are books of Prophecy.

5. 1 (xiii) *God's Faith (or Zeal)*

At the same speed He spoke, He created the heavens and the earth. That God is able is a tested fact – His faith in His Word created the heavens and the earth. He has also planted in His children the ability, zeal, and faith that is inside of Him so that we may be able to repossess all corners of the earth for His glory. That is vision for the children of God. It is left for individual believers and the church to rediscover the plan (the Lord's plan for His own) to reclaim the earth for Jesus.

God's Faith is in His Word; His heart and conscience (that is, the big circle which represents Jesus Christ in *The Prophecy Box*) would achieve His purposes. *Personal prophecies* are products of

5.0 The Prophecy Box

God's zeal, belief and faith that He will accomplish what He has promised. Isaiah 9: 7 says that the zeal of the Lord Almighty will accomplish the birth of King Jesus Christ. Between the Old Testament and New Testament was 400 years of unrecorded history. But it happened. This is *Prophecy*! It is God's zeal that accomplishes God's promises. What is God's zeal and faith? Him! The effective power of His Holy Spirit.

5.1 (xiv) Jesus is the Light shining in the dark place

Jesus Christ is the true light that gives light to every man who comes into the world (John 1: 9). For the earth and the minds of men are being stolen and controlled by Lucifer since the time he was banished from the camp of God, and condemned to hell to rot. He possesses the heart of men that would want to do evil. But there is hope in Jesus, the lamb slain before the foundations of the earth. Jesus is the light shining in the dark place (the earth, which He created at the same speed He spoke). John 1: 1–5 says, 'In the beginning was the Word, and the Word was with God, and the Word was God. He was with God in the beginning. Through Him all things were made; without Him nothing was made that has been made. In Him was life, and that life was the light of men. The light shines in the darkness, but the darkness has not understood it.' It's a mandate and a clarion call that we have to turn the hearts of men back to God all over the land and all over the world: the poor in spirit and those rich in material things in top businesses, in the commanding heights of every economy on the surface of the earth (for instance, in Oil, Shipping, Finance, Academia etc.). Then we will be strategically claiming the earth back for God. Then we can say proudly, 'Christian believers own the world because we are called to own the world'. For if it is written, the land and everything in it is of God, surely it must be of God and of His only Son Jesus Christ. The bigger circle in the box represents Jesus Christ – the light shining in the dark place, and also explains theoretically why Christ must be preached in all corners and ends of the earth.

5.0 The Prophecy Box

5.1 (xv) The Master's Call

The Prophecy Box also describes the Master's call of His chosen children for work of service for Him. For we were formed and summoned by God (Isaiah 43: 1). We are God's witnesses on earth called to do His will for His own glory (Isaiah 43: 10).

Our Master (God) draws His chosen ones to Himself through different experiences, situations and stages in life. Every good and bad situation must bring *Israel* back to God.

Prophecy is like a call for service you never have a complete picture of: What do I mean? We learn new things about God every day and we cannot know Him fully until Jesus Christ returns, and so also *personal prophecies* can come in fragments and directions are granted in stages. Time to respond to *personal prophecy* and act upon *personal prophecy* must be appropriate. For example, concerning King David's prophetic call for service – until David received the Priestly anointing, he was just the leader of Israel.

Abraham had a call to leave Canaan for a more prosperous land where he will put himself to work and his hands will bear good fruit in the land of milk and honey. He left Canaan for a purpose; he knew he was still going to work in the Promised Land (since Adam and Eve's sin, man had been told by God he will have to toil and struggle before he eats), but his toil will be worthwhile. The Israelites toil everywhere (today all over the world), and their engagements have always been worthwhile, +++ every time they obeyed God. In fact, I strongly believe, personally, that to date they have been the most prosperous and enterprising human race since creation. Abraham did not follow God blindly: there was a vision and a purpose which was realised. When the Master called Abraham and he received the vision by faith, he set about realising the vision and purpose to prosper in another land.

Faith is about vision and purpose (for example, a mission abroad to meet the needs of unprivileged people and in the process win souls for Christ), and achieving and realising that vision and purpose. We as Christians must know that 'He who is the portion of Jacob… for He is the Maker of all things including Israel, the tribe of his inheritance – the Lord Almighty is his name' – He will fulfil all things when he sends us and reveals a 'game plan' for His chosen ones. And that is *Prophecy!*

5.1 (xvi) The Christian's Life Experience (Christ's Experience on Earth)

The Prophecy Box also describes the Christian's life experience. The Christian's life experience is akin to Christ's earthly experience. Christ's life involved suffering and struggle. And struggle is about rising up to every challenge and overcoming. A Christian must rise up to every challenge and prove Christ in Him – we are born to win. Believers must win as Christ won when He defeated the enemy – He descended into hell to disdain the enemy and later resurrected in victory and then ascended into heaven after the storm. For Christ said we shall face many struggles but He will be with us. John 16: 33 says, 'I have told you these things, so that in me you may have peace. In this world you will have trouble. But take heart! I have overcome the world.'

I have personally experienced in my inner man Christ's anointing so strong that He released inner strength and boldness in the face of storms, unbearable struggles, pain, deceit, betrayal and obstacles. Overcoming the tumultuous experience I consider the delivering power of God.

Overcoming and winning does not mean losing God's fruit of the spirit (for example, self-control, love, patience, perseverance, humility) in the face of turmoil and storm – for Christ's other name is Peace. In a troubled world devoid of peace where it is so easy to hate when offended and aggrieved, you must decide to love by the grace of the Holy Spirit without bitterness and rancour after all – that, if achieved, I will consider miraculous! This is putting the enemy in his rightful position – condemned and irrelevant, and he will not have a part of you through bitterness, pain, hatred, revenge and grief.

It is a fact of life that after a war there should be rest or peace. The peace process may sometimes be slow, but there should be peace eventually after every war. So it is with every turmoil, storm, trouble, humiliation, failure in life. When you remain steadfast in the Lord through perseverance, patience and love instead of being bitter, you are able to go through fire without being consumed by the circumstance and the event. The aftermath of the event bears good fruits in you. The tangible fruits of love, perseverance and patience may not be immediately apparent but they will show up eventually. And there is also the opportunity of rebuilding and reconciliation. When we go through the refiner's fire or are salted by fire successfully by God, we become stronger and well prepared to receive new blessings coupled with the ability to keep those blessings. Even when the struggles, storm and pain are God's act as a result of disobedience, there is a historical precedent in the word of God that the almighty God will not be angry with *Israel* forever. His mercies will endure forever!

Life's experience and God's wrath must bring us back to Him. As every fierce war should lead eventually to peace, so with God, the Christian-believer's experience of God's wrath must lead to obedience, and subsequently something good (for instance, blessings, favour, love etc.) (Deut. 28: 1-14). For this is the reality of the Christian's experience! Life is difficult but He has overcome! This is *Prophecy!*

5.1 (xvii) The Prophets' Experience

The Prophecy Box describes the Prophets of Israel's experience with their people, which was akin to the experience of God with His people as their leader, and the experience of Jesus Christ His Son as our Saviour. The images portrayed of the Spirit and ways of God of dealing with His people by the characters, the clockwise patterned four mini-boxes (Man→ Prophet(s)→ Jesus Christ→ Holy Spirit) within the Prophecy Box are similar. The Prophets of old heard from the source of life – the Almighty God and the source of all Prophets. God dwelt amongst His people and ruled the people through the Judges and Prophets He sent. It was the same cry of atonement and salvation. Some of the Prophets like Isaiah and Jeremiah gave personal prophecies about the coming of the Messiah the source of life (God coming in flesh to earth) to redeem His people of sin. The Messiah was addressed as 'Rabbi' or a Prophet by His disciples – the Prophet of all Prophets and source of the Prophets. He was meant to die in flesh so that His Holy Spirit might forever live in those who believe in Him.

Reiterating, we can explain the Prophet's experience with the circle within *The Prophecy Box*. Within the circle are four mini-boxes referred to as *Man, Prophet(s) Jesus Christ and the Holy Spirit* respectively, and in each box dwells the complete image and spirit of God. Each box (where we have *Man, Prophet(s) Jesus Christ and the Holy Spirit)* exemplifies the authority and love of God for that which He created particularly at various historical periods. The last three (prophet(s), Jesus Christ and the Holy Spirit) play the role of redemption and salvation for the people. Now we are in the season of the outpouring of the Holy Spirit (God's power and anointing) on those who have found and received Him by His grace.

As we travel clockwise from one mini-box to another *(Man→ Prophet(s) →Jesus →Christ →Holy Spirit)* we observe the sovereignty of the three-in-one person, which is God the Father, God the Son and God the Holy Spirit. Summarily, the entire big circle can be referred to as Jesus Christ, which therefore reconfirms the claim in the preparation model that the big circle represents Jesus Christ. The prophetic pattern of God has always been consistent over the ages.

5.1 (xviii) The Concept of Judgement

It is possible to use *The Prophecy Box* to explain some of the profound and confounding statements and truths of Jesus Christ. For example, *judging others*. Matt. 7: 1–2 says, 'Do not judge, or you too will be judged. For in the same way as you judge others, you will be judged, and with the measure you use, it will be measured to you.' *The Prophecy Box* shows why we must not judge others (not always). For example judgement has been the bane of misunderstanding and disunity amongst Christian denominations. The *Prophecy Box* states that Jesus Christ is present everywhere on earth as portrayed pictorially by the big circle. And if we sincerely believe that this is true and that God is present in all places at the same time, then there will be no need of judging others' actions, because God can discern. Without judgement, peace is bound to reign in the Church and then we can speak with a common voice. The idea of individuals and Churches judging one another becomes unproductive, and has repercussions when we decide to do otherwise and to play the role of God. The moment we judge, we open ourselves to judgement by other people who may want to evaluate the correctness of our judgement. Judgement (correct or incorrect?) sometimes leads to avoidable cracks in our integrity and trustworthiness. Untainted, incontestable and righteous judgement only belongs to and come from the Lord. For God is present in all places at the same time – omnipresent. He alone must remain the judge.

I believe the God we serve is an awesome God who is able to witness to the hearts of men in every situation. Although He is a God who sometimes takes His time, He does act. I do not support the contamination of the Word of God. For the Church must dwell in Spirit, and in a spiritual sense it is important for the Church of today to seek the Lord and go to the Word of God in ironing out differences amongst themselves, even when we still have to resolve some issues. There must be a balance between the issues we deal with as individuals and what should be left to God. I would rather give judgement and decisions about situations I have been given authority and control of by God, rather than give judgement on one I do not have authority or control over.

Let us live in the Spirit and agree on what is written and undiluted in the true Word of God. Do not judge (not always), for judgement belongs to the Lord – so it is written! During the promotion of my first book, *The A–Z Model of the Word,* I discovered that one of the banes of the disunity within the body of Christ is as a result of each denomination believing each has the monopoly of the Word and Word of God and therefore of the Truth therein. Before God there are no denominations, and as we continue to work out our salvation individually, only Christ knows those who have already made it to heaven and will make it to heaven. It is important for each denomination not to judge one another always – do not judge for judgement belongs to the Lord. This is *Prophecy!*

Therefore, with the design of *The Prophecy Box* and the truth of Christ described and proven therein, many other fundamental statements and issues pertaining to the position of the Trinity can be explained.

5.1 (xix) Spiritual Location of the Word of God

This is akin to the subject of Geography and can be called *Spiritual*

5.0 The Prophecy Box

Geography (SG). The Prophecy Box describes the location of God in the Universe, and in the affairs of men in the land of the living. God is omnipresent – present in all places at the same time. The boundaries of the box called God's Love can be likened to the boundaries of the universe, and the big circle in the box regarded as Jesus Christ can be likened to the earth we live in. The Holy Spirit permeates all areas of the universe (including the heavens and the earth). As we cannot take the earth away from the universe so we cannot take Jesus Christ (who is the heart and conscience of the Almighty God) away from His father.

Let us compare the activities of the humanist (for example, Greenpeace, Environmentalists and Conservationists) to activities of the Christian believers in the propagation of the Gospel of Jesus Christ within the subject of SG. As Greenpeace, Conservationists, and the Environmentalists strive to preserve the earth from destruction by Man, Christian-believers as followers of Jesus Christ are chosen to preserve God's Word by ministering the Word and bringing people to Christ. To be involved in Greenpeace involves a deep awareness, knowledge and love for the environment, and for Christian believers to be involved at the cutting edge without being blunted in the ministration of the Word and winning of souls for Christ in this generation will involve a deep knowledge and awareness of God and what He says He is in His Word. This is achieved through being holy and His unmerited favour – blessing, love, mercy and grace. Analogously, as Greenpeace strive to achieve their course by physical means (for instance, sometimes through physical aggression), so do Christian-believers, Prophets, Teachers, Evangelists and men of God prepare their bodies and souls and receive from God in the spirit realm (for instance, through spiritual warfare prayer). For it is written in Matt. 11: 12 that since the days of John the Baptist, the kingdom of heaven has been suffering violence, and the violent have had to claim it by force.

As the earth continues to revolve on its axis, so will the written word of God (or Jesus Christ revealed as the big circle in *The Prophecy Box*) continue to revolve round every generation for all time, sustained by God's Love for ever. For it is written in Psalm 138: 2 by King David that, '…for your love and your faithfulness, for you have exalted above all things your name and your word'.

Just as Astronauts travel into space in order to gain more insight and knowledge, so Theologians, Pentecostals, Bible Commentators, Writers, Prophets, and anointed men of God through their spirituality receive the secret things of God for better and deeper understanding of Him.

5.1 (xx) Rebuking and Training Process

In abstract terms *The Prophecy Box* reveals the rebuking and training pattern in man-God relationship since the beginning to the end (from Genesis to Revelation). As the box describes every experience since creation and the nature and pattern of man-God relationship since Adam and Eve to the close of the age, it also gives an authoritative source of correction, way of hope, comfort, peace, direction, redemption and salvation. The Rebuking and Training Process (RTP) reveals the necessity for obedience and faithfulness, and indicates a pathway to God's blessings, favour, love, eternity and all the good things associated with God (2 Tim. 3: 16–17), which is through Christ at the centre of the Prophecy Box. This we can also deduce from issues discussed before now. All scriptures are good for training and so are *personal prophecies.*

To put the RTP simply, the written word of God from Genesis to Revelation is useful for training and rebuking, so are *personal prophecies* received. It may be a word of caution about the way you live (for instance, no sex outside marriage, and obeying the laws of God).

5.1 (xxi) Timing and Consistency

Prophecy (or *personal prophecy*) is not limited by time, and any perceived delays must inevitably bring us back to Him. It is written that we should seek first the kingdom of God and His righteousness and every other thing shall be added to it. Even before the foundations of the world were laid, Jesus Christ was the lamb slain to restore His children to their perfect state. His anointing is capable of restoring to that perfect whole that which we have lost in due time. God's timing may not necessarily be our timing, yet God is never late but always on time.

5.0 The Prophecy Box

From the time of Noah to the end of the Old Testament was two thousand years. Another four hundred years lapsed between the Old Testament and the New Testament. There was no recorded history of the Israelites. The time-span between the prophetic messages of Isaiah (in the Old Testament) about the coming of John the Baptist and Jesus Christ the Messiah (in the New Testament) and the actual realisation of those prophecies must have been longer than four hundred years. *Prophecy* (and *personal prophecies*) can take time: four hundred years is long indeed for the coming of Jesus Christ! And when personal prophecy manifests, it is the hand of God revealed in the physical realm.

For thousands of years since creation God has been reconciling His people to himself out of love. He has always been consistent. He has always done it (for instance, through Noah, His Prophets, Jesus Christ), and now through His Holy Spirit. He never gives up on us, and always proves His word. Habakkuk 2: 2–4 states, 'Then the Lord replied: Write down the revelation and make it plain on tablets so that a herald may run with it. For the revelation awaits an appointed time; it speaks of the end and will not prove false. Though it linger, wait for it; it will certainly come and will not delay.'

God's blessings in His timing must bring us back to Him.

5.1 (xxii) Prophecy is about Testimony.

Testimony is about the end-result of the prophetic word of God. It describes God's ability to perform His word. Testimony goes one stage further to declare that God has done it. The operative word(s) being *declare/make known* to the world. It is about vision and prophetic statements realised, and the unfailing word of God concerning His own children and unbelievers living under His benevolence and grace. Jehovah is a God of promise(s) fulfilled. The word of God shall not return to Him without accomplishing that which He has destined to achieve. The prophetic word of God is about the realisation of the promises of God. God never fails.

Several examples of prophetic statements and testimonies permeate the Holy Bible from Genesis to Revelation. The births of John the Baptist and of Jesus Christ were prophesied in the book of Prophet Isaiah in the Old Testament and these were revealed hundreds of years later in the New Testament. There were also examples of barren women who were provided children after receiving the prophetic word of God such as Hannah (1 Samuel 2: 1–11), Sarah (Genesis 11: 30), Rebekah (Genesis 25: 21), Rachel (Genesis 29: 31) and Elizabeth (Luke 1: 7). Though it tarries, it must come to pass. Christians own the world.

5. 1 (xxiii) Prophets

Prophets are those with the prophetic anointing. They are God's messengers, and serve as guardians onto the path of knowledge and truth. For Prophets are known to rebuke and to restore the children of God to the path of restoration. Jesus was also addressed as a *Prophet* – 'Rabbi' (Mk. 9: 5). He was the source of the Prophets. For it is said that a Prophet is a lone voice in the wilderness. In our generation, God's Prophets must not become lone voices in the wilderness!

Jesus was the ideal Prophet without any sin. He was a *child of Prophecy* and born of prophetic word of love by His father for the world. Jesus Christ was God's Love – His only begotten Son that He gave to the world. Simon Peter speaking on the *prophecy of Scripture* and God's Love (2 Peter 1: 16–21) said, 'We did not follow cleverly invented stories when we told you about the power and coming of our Lord Jesus Christ, but we were eye-witnesses of His majesty. For He received honour and glory from God the Father when the voice came to Him from the Majestic glory, saying, 'This is my Son, whom I love; with Him I am well pleased.' We ourselves heard this voice that came from heaven when we were with Him on the sacred mountain.'

And Peter continued, 'And we have the word of the Prophets made more certain, and you will do well to pay attention to it, as to a light shining in the dark, until the day dawns and the morning star rises in your hearts. Above all, you must understand that no prophecy of Scripture came about by the prophet's own interpretation. For prophecy never had its origin in the will of man, but men spoke from God as they were carried along by the Holy Spirit.'

Prophecy is about the Holy Spirit, and the anointing that reveals all knowledge to mankind¹. As we cannot understand the length, breadth, width and height of God and His love, so also we cannot determine the length, breadth, width and height of Prophecy and God's prophecies in the Christian life. It is a continuous process, we keep learning. Interpretation and wisdom of discerning of personal prophecies can only be gained through continuous fellowship with the Holy Spirit and by striving for holiness.

5.1 (xxiv) False Personal Prophecies

A text on false teachers and their destruction is in 2 Peter 2. And the Bible text on testing if a spirit is from God is found in 1 John 4: 1–6. *As there are false prophets, there are false spirits ruling the false prophets: they work hand in hand.*

It is possible for *The Prophecy Box* to be permeated by evil and false spirits. It is only the anointing and power of God that will overwhelm and overcome the spiritual oppression and injustice of the enemy. I discovered in the summer months of 1995 that holiness powered by the Holy Ghost is the key to receiving God's anointing that will destroy the yoke of the enemy and release God's healing, deliverance, blessings and favour. Ultimately, holiness (for instance, righteousness of God) and false spirits will not work together: the former will have to displace the latter through the blood of Jesus Christ.

When we meditate more on His prophetic word (in the physical realm through the reading of the Holy Bible), we can understand with clarity what the Holy Spirit is revealing in the spirit realm. With adequate consumption of the word of God, we can discern false messengers and false messages. As we draw nearer to God in holiness and wait upon Him for direction we move from the physical into the spirit realm into the presence of God, and it becomes clearer to decipher Godly-prophecies from false prophecies. Moses and Jesus fasted for forty days and forty nights, and the purposes and intentions of God became clearer to them. We do not move from the spirit to the physical in the first instance, only God of the heavens who resides there does so. Prophets of God and Christians move from the word of God in

---

[1] I learnt it was the source of early scientists like Copernicus, Pascal, Kepler, Galileo who were also Christians in Charles Colson's *Unity of the Body*.

the physical realm into the spirit realm and not otherwise. 'Powers' that move from the spirit realm to the physical realm in the first instance are evil.

Though evil spirits permeate both the heavens (spirit realm and thus our dreams) and the earth (Physical realm which is sometimes witnessed in our individual daily endeavours). 'For our struggle is not against flesh and blood, but against the rulers, against the authorities, against the powers of this dark world and against the spiritual forces of evil in the heavenly realms' (Ephesians 6: 12). It is therefore important to put on the full armour of God (Ephesians 6: 10–20), which is Jesus Christ (representing the specific areas covered by the armour). Above all, the grace and the love of God overcomes evil and all fear.

Therefore, as we receive more of God's love and anointing, *personal prophecies* received resemble more accurately the word (proclaimed by the Scriptures) and Word of God Jesus Christ. *Therefore, once personal prophecy is outside the word of God (and extends beyond the divine promises of God which are a product of obedience to the word and the Word) there is reason to object to any such personal prophecy.* It will be deceptive. For instance if you stop meditating on the word of God in your daily life, it is only true that the devil will permeate the *personal prophecies* you receive and, ultimately; will begin to give you his own *personal prophecies. Particularly to Christian-believers who revel in dreams – it is best to rely more on the Word than dreams.*

There must be a dynamic balance and safeguard in messages received through dreams and which should corroborate the facts revealed in the word of God. As a safeguard let us rely more on the written word of God. This is not anomalistic to the truth of the Scriptures about Godly-dreams received by Joseph, Daniel and other great men of God which were a contributing factor in their narrow path to success. Godly-dreams are God-personified.

I have read and heard that a Prophet can only confirm that which the Lord has spoken to us individually in the first instance. Personally, I believe Prophets are also meant to give fresh information to us. Prophets of old like Isaiah did consistently reveal the coming of the Son of God to the world (unto us a child is born [Isaiah 9]). That Truth who is Jesus Christ came to the world hundreds of years later. But, practically, I would prefer that we continuously pray that the word of God come alive in our lives and give us direction rather than hang on to deceptive spirits, pronouncements, voices and adulterous Prophets which we are never sure about.

5. 1 (xxv) Concept of Continuity

Prophecy (and personal prophecies) are continuous as both the Old Testament and New Testament are one long continuous cyclical prophetic story and are one, about the central subject which is Jesus Christ who has given His prophetic word to mankind. The Lord God's dominion is both in the physical realm and the spirit realm which He has separated by His own design. He formed both the earth and the heavens for His own glory. Jesus Christ is the Word, who spoke and revealed His word (both in the Old Testament and New Testament) to transform and reconcile His people to Him. From the foundation of the world to the close of the age, Jesus is all God wanted to say to us on earth. And until the light which is Jesus and His prophetic word shines into the deep darkness of our heart and throughout the earth, we will never understand the deep meaning of *personal prophecies* we receive, and the course of our vision.

Personal prophecy on any significant or major event in our life would be continuous whether we acknowledge the prophetic message and/or Prophets or not. The Lord is consistent; He will continue to visit you to assert that His faith will do it. He is faithful even when we are unfaithful. The coming of Jesus was a continuous prophetic message by Prophet Isaiah (Isaiah 7, 9, 11). Every new prophetic message about the same subject must reinforce and reassert the first claim that He is faithful and will do that which He has promised to do. Every prophetic message re-asserts and re-intensifies God's love.

As the prophetic word of God – Old and New Testament – are continuous, so personal prophecies (i.e. through the written word of God (the Holy Bible), spoken word through prophets, visions and dreams) concerning our lives will be a continuous process. Until the deepness and integrity of Jesus Christ enter our hearts through His word,' then will His light completely shine into the deep darkness of our hearts. Otherwise, we will never understand the deep meaning of personal prophecies we receive, the course of our visions and even the sources sometimes.

As we consciously and continuously work out our salvation, we continuously learn to get our personal prophecies right. We make mistakes along the long walk about sources and interpretation, but we learn to get them right, through the opening of our eyes by the anointing of the Holy Spirit about the deep things of the spirit world at the appropriate time. God would always do the real thing over and over again. For example, while speaking to the Ephesian elders of the Church at his farewell, Paul said, 'And now, compelled by the Spirit, I am going to Jerusalem…' (Acts 20: 22). However, at Caesarea on the way to Jerusalem, a Prophet named Agabus came down from Judea. Took Paul's belt, tied his own hands and feet with it and said, 'The Holy Spirit says, "In this way the Jews of Jerusalem will bind the owner of this belt and will hand him over to the Gentiles".' When Paul's associates like Luke and the other people with them heard this, they all pleaded with Paul not to go up to Jerusalem. Agabus' personal prophecy was misinterpreted. It was true that Paul would be bound, but it was not true that he should not go to Jerusalem (Acts 21: 10–12). When Paul would not be dissuaded, Luke and the rest gave up and said, 'The Lord's will be done' (Acts 21: 14). The same experience happened to Jesus with His disciples, we all learn as we work out our salvation.

5.1 (xxvi) Literature and Prophecy Compared

As we cannot take the work of William Shakespeare away from the study of modern English literature, so we cannot take the prophetic writings, teachings, patterns and literary style of the Prophets away from the word of God. It would lead to reduction of the truth of the Word. Thus the word of God from Genesis to Revelation would become incomplete.

5.1 (xxvii) The Word is Prophecy

The Word is Prophecy is saying God is God (or who He says He is), and His sovereignty remains in a dark world. In abstract terms (explaining using *The Prophecy Box*) the bigger circle represents the Word that is Jesus Christ – the Son of God. And Jesus Christ is also God the Father in flesh. Therefore the bigger circle also represents God, and God's presence and sovereignty on the earth we live in. The bigger circle in the box or the Word also represents the written word of God from Genesis to Revelation. All creation lives under the benevolence of God. Therefore, we are justified to say that the bigger circle is God. In abstract terms, What is *Prophecy? Prophecy is the written word of God from Genesis to Revelation and that is about the Trinity (God the Father; God the Son and God the Holy Spirit) as proven in The Prophecy Box*. Therefore, in abstract terms, *The Word is Prophecy* proves that God is God: God in the middle (the bigger circle) and God represented by the outer square-shaped boundary (called God's Love). The boundaries of the box and all therein represent all the names of God and existence past and present, proving that God's sovereignty remains in the heavens and the earth.

I believe The Prophecy Box has the potential of discussing every issue that pertains to life and death so far as God the author of the blueprint gives the revelation knowledge to the reader.

The spirit of God and Christianity cannot be *compartmentalised*, it must get beyond *religion* (man's way to God) and *dogma* (unquestionable belief). *The Prophecy Box* proves this accurately with the various concepts, and that Christianity embraces all facets of society, and all human's professions and subjects around which our world functions. I believe it is possible to tap into the abundant treasures of God as we come to Jesus Christ to seek knowledge and wisdom in a way we have never known before. The idea that Jesus Christ must be at the centre of every enterprise, excellence and knowledge is unalienable. Commitment to Jesus Christ first, and every other knowledge will follow. Jesus is the source and giver of all Godly- knowledge and creative talents and inventions that have shaped the world, particularly present western civilization. Most early scientists were also Christians and so were many early citadels of academia. There was a time when Christian faith and investment in educational excellence and invention were inseparable. It was during the 17th century that opinion changed and that separated *faith* and *reason*;

and control of thought became independent of the Church[1]. The word and Word of God gave birth to all excellence, creativity and all forms of art and science. For the Lord owns the earth. It is better for Christians to study Church history and to find out how we missed His Truth (the Truth about the trend and pattern of western civilization which initially originated from Christian foundational truth centuries back) than to continue daily to proclaim ignorantly and daily that the world's institutions belong to Satan (or at best were always secular) as if it has always and would forever be. Over the years Satan and his agents continue to bend the truth and they are still bending the truth.

The Word is Prophecy. Jesus is *Prophecy* (*a continuous Prophecy gone in flesh and coming back*)! The spirit of Jesus is *Prophecy*. The spirit of Jesus is the spirit of empowerment, order, destiny and authority that sustains the universe. Jesus remains sovereign and is coming soon in His mighty power to restore His own in this dark world. For it is written in the book of Revelation 22: 7, 'Behold I am coming soon! Blessed is he who keeps the words of the prophecy in this book...' Indeed, He shall come soon in person and no longer will He exist in a mystical sense as He does presently. *The Word is Prophecy.* God is God, however, while we wait *His sovereignty remains in a dark world.*

---

[1] Charles Colson's *Unity of the Body* and Avery Dulles' *Model of the Church* overwhelmingly confirmed my thoughts about compatibility of *Faith and Reason*, and the contributions the Christian faith had made to education and western civilization over the centuries. Whatever doubts I had disappeared after reading these books.

6.0 The Prophecy Box Further Elaborated and Explained

The Prophecy Box is further elaborated and tested using the *concepts of visualisation and realisation* and *reduction and restoration*. A test to prove if *The Prophecy Box* stands as a Christian theological model could be proven through these two methods: (i) *visualisation and realisation* and (ii) *reduction and restoration*. Both (i) and (ii) prove the acceptability of *The Prophecy Box* as a Christian theological model that works, and that the Word of God is an integrated whole.

6.1 METHOD OF VISUALISATION AND REALISATION

The first method of *Prophecy* is visualisation (that is generation, imagination, conception and origination[1]) in the spiritual realm of an event that is going to occur in the future, and then the existence and realisation of that occurrence in the physical realm. *The beginning and end of Prophecy is making the unseen with the natural eye seen in the physical.*

Prophecy in the context of the word of God, and every act of God from creation and supposedly to the close of the age share the same Godly footprints, style, process, method, plan and design. There is always *a time of visualisation* (that is conception, imagination, generation) of an idea in the spirit, and then the Lord brings into existence and realisation the idea in the physical realm.

For example, the act of creation by God in the beginning was an act of *Prophecy*. In Genesis 1: 1 we are told, 'In the beginning, God created the heavens and the earth'. In the process of creating the heavens and earth, God must have *visualised* (that is imagined, designed, planned and conceived) a picture of the heavens and earth He wanted to create in the spirit, before bringing into existence the realization of His design. This recorded act of

---

[1] These are synonyms given by the Oxford Dictionary of the English Language.

creation of heavens and earth, that is moving from *visualization* (that is imagination) and then bringing into existence and realisation the heavens and earth, I consider God's prophetic style and method, and God's first prophetic act known to man, although this action was swift. This *prophetic style of visualization* and imagination, and then bringing into existence was also present in the creation of Man. Genesis 1: 26–27 declares, 'Then God said, 'Let us make man in our image, in our likeness...' So God created man in His own image, in the image of God He created him; male and female He created them.' God conceived the idea of creating man in the spirit before He gave birth to Him in the physical realm. The book of Revelation 13: 8 referred to the Old Testament statement that Jesus was the lamb slain from the creation of the world. This was not manifested and realised in the physical until the New Testament. That was a very long period – *personal prophecies* take time.

As complex as the vision of creation may sound, it is *written*. The vision and purpose of God from the beginning to the end is written in the Holy Bible, and that vision of God is what we, as Christian-believers, pursue every day. The ultimate goal is to fulfil the vision and purpose of God *written* since Ancient of days to reconcile man to Him. Every church of God must have a *written vision*: a vision that Christian-believers can run with and which will serve as a means and tool of adding more people to the kingdom. The vision must be *testable* and *quantifiable*. It must be possible to check from time to time to see that they are in line and in tune with their aims, goals and purposes. It is important we discover our God-given *vision* and talents through the Holy Spirit, and also paramount that we have the vision written. *If we designed one independent of God for ourselves it is ambition: that is a goal designed and driven by flesh. I believe there is a God-given vision for every Christian-believer.*

However, some human deeds have served mankind well. Do we call this vision? When Christians have been found wanting, secular men have been used to achieve God's purposes. Whilst the South African Churches were napping, Nelson Mandela, the president of South Africa, wrote down his 'vision' for a parliamentary democratic South Africa where Africans and those

6.0 The Prophecy Box Further Elaborated and Explained

of European descent would be treated as equals. I remember in secondary school reading Nelson Mandela's treasonable felony trial manuscripts titled, 'The struggle is my life', where he clearly stated he was willing to die for the cause (his vision for a free South Africa)[1]. Even though he was in prison for twenty-seven years, South African youths and other freedom fighters around the world that were born in his prison years did not rely only on hearsay about Mandela's 'vision' for a free South Africa, they also had access to his written word and plan, 'The struggle is my life', and other books written by him about his cause. Even though the latter-day youths and revolutionaries never saw Nelson Mandela in the flesh, it was the acceptability of his written 'vision' and identification with his cause that propelled and drove them (including the likes of the late Steve Biko). It is also sad to note that it was (one of us!) a church-reverend and later prime minister of South Africa that promulgated the apartheid policy into law. *A man, a church and society without vision will abuse God-given objects. A gift without purpose become a gift of abuse. God created everything for a purpose.*

The Church today must be a Church of vision, purpose and destiny powered and directed by the Holy Ghost to make a difference in our society for the good of mankind and not a religious Church dead and irrelevant to the world. Churches and Christian-believers that would play at the cutting edge in ministry, mission and marketplace must have a vision, a mission and a written purpose for existence and operation.

Like little seeds that grow and become a forest, vision grows and the mission is realised. This would require step(s) of faith. The process of growth may be difficult and this issue of difficulty leads us to the second method of God, the method of reduction to restoration. Just as Nelson Mandela has frequently said, particularly during the negotiating process and electioneering campaign (and also on the cover of his biography), the path to

---

[1] This was given to me when I was a young schoolboy at about age twelve by my Dad, John Jemine Adollo, an ebullient journalist and former editor of a Nigerian national newspaper. Most of the best books that have shaped my thoughts and thinking are those I read in my father's home library and those handed to me by him.

freedom and victory (or any other good cause and Godly vision) is not usually an easy walk. Realisation eventually took place after the vision and dream of a free South Africa.

6.2 METHOD OF REDUCTION AND RESTORATION

6.2 (i) Restoration

God's ultimate plan for man (since the time Adam and Eve committed the first sin) has been to restore man to his proper and rightful place with Him. God's prophecies' are also meant ultimately to restore (that is plant, redeem) us into our rightful positions, bring to birth His promises and blessings. He is a God that remedies every situation.

God always sent a remedy both in the Old Testament and in the New Testament in the form of His chosen Prophets (*Rabbi*) to whom He gave specific calling and anointing, and finally, through the coming of the Messiah for complete redemption. Some of His Prophets were Moses, Elijah and Isaiah. Elijah and Jesus were both rejected and restored. When Jesus' disciples asked Him, 'Why do the teachers of the law say that Elijah must come first?' Jesus replied, 'To be sure, Elijah does come first, and restores all things. Why then is it written that the Son of Man must suffer much and be rejected? But I tell you Elijah has come, and they have done to him everything they wished, just as it is written about him' (Mk. 9: 11–12).

The Prophecy Box captures the restoration and redemption experience as well. In the Old Testament, God created man in His own very perfect image and likeness (that is, His spirit) with full power and anointing, and with total authority to control His domain (Genesis 1: 26–31). The Holy Spirit put man in the Garden of Eden. In the middle of the garden were the tree of life and the tree of the knowledge of good and evil (Gen. 2: 9). And the Lord God said, 'You are free to eat from any tree in the garden; but you must not eat from the tree of knowledge of good and evil, for when you eat of it you will surely die' (Genesis 2: 17). And then the fall of man – he broke the first covenant. He ate from the tree of unnecessary knowledge to discover and experience for himself good and evil (Gen. 3: 6). After the Lord God drove man out, He placed on the east side of the Garden of Eden cherubim and a flaming sword flashing back and forth to guard the way to the tree of life (Genesis 3: 24). Of the tree of life and immortality man can no longer eat. Man was reconciled back to God by the promise of the new seed – Jesus Christ – in the New Testament. Revelation 2:7 says, 'He who has an ear, let him hear what the Spirit says to the churches. To him who overcomes, I will give the right to eat from the tree of life, which is in the paradise of God.' Revelation 22: 2 says, 'down the middle of the great street of the city. On each side of the river stood the tree of life, bearing twelve crops of fruit, yielding its fruit every month. And the leaves of the tree are for the healing of the nations.' Jesus is the tree of life, and the Holy Spirit restores our perfect manhood in the likeness of God.

6.2 (ii) Reduction

Some *personal prophecies* reduce and humble us, but the end result is *restoration* and elevation. Therefore, we will ask why do we sometimes receive messages from the Holy Spirit that do not reveal and say good things about future events concerning us?

6.3 WHY ARE WE REDUCED?

Since Adam and Eve we have lived in a world of sin and mortality. And the Holy Spirit is saying, the event may occur which sometimes does even when we pray; but I am with you. Initially, we may be *reduced* and unhappy about that which was revealed, but ultimately we will be blessed, elevated and restored to our rightful position. Jesus was *reduced* on earth. He was sorrowful and troubled when going to the cross, and He prayed in Matthew 26: 39, 'My Father, if it is possible, may this cup be taken from me. Yet not as I will, but as you will.' He would have loved not to go through the humiliating experience, but had to go through the agonising death for us to be freed and rescued, especially from the sin of old.

Thus, *Prophecy* as shown by the word of God from Genesis to Revelation may sometimes be accompanied by reduction before restoration and elevation. Joseph's brothers *reduced* Joseph before he was restored and elevated by God; Haman planned evil against Mordecai before he was *restored* and elevated by the king; and Judas Iscariot *reduced* Jesus Christ before He was restored and elevated. *To be reduced, restored and elevated is the reality of the Christian life.*

6.4 HOW DO WE DEAL WITH REDUCTIVE PROPHECIES?

We deal with *reductive prophecies* by searching for the truth of God. We search for the truth by *living holy lives,* which enable God to outpour His anointing upon our lives. And definitely, the anointing will destroy the yoke and smother the enemy. *Being holy is living according to the standards of God.* No other book in the Bible lays more emphasis on the word *Holy* than the book of Revelation. Being holy is synonymous to Godliness, and is the paramount rule and key for all blessings.

6.4 (i) Word of God

At the heart of God is His word (His Sword). To know the word of God is about discerning the Almighty God's heart and principles. Indeed, it is important we know the Holy Bible. Studying the Holy Bible (not literally but spiritually calling on the Holy Spirit for guidance) and believing the Holy Bible (from Genesis to Revelation). Being *holy* and pure and purification are based on obeying the truth of the Word of God, and accepting that Jesus is Lord and over all. 1 Peter 1: 22 states that 'For you have been born again, not of perishable seed, but of imperishable, through the living and enduring Word of God'.

It is better we begin to study the Word of God with our spiritual eyes and mind for the message, truth and power of God to be effectively appropriated. This will be effectively achieved as we seek the grace of the Holy Spirit in prayer before studying the Word.

6.4 (ii) Meditation

Meditation on the word of God is also important, just as God instructed Joshua. Joshua 1: 8 says, 'Do not let this Book of Law depart from your mouth; meditate on it day and night, so that you may be careful to do everything written in it. Then you will be prosperous and successful.'

6.4 (iii) The Human Body as the Temple of God

Our body is God's dwelling place and we have to live as living sacrifices recognising that it represents the Temple of God. Romans 12:1 states, '...offer your bodies as living sacrifices, *holy* and pleasing to God – this is your spiritual act of worship. Do not conform any longer to the pattern of this world, but be transformed by the renewing of your mind. Then you will be able to test and approve what God's will is – His good, pleasing and perfect will.'

It is important that we sanctify and season by the Holy Spirit every liquid and solid (that is food) that we eat each day, accepting them as sacrifices of thanksgiving and blessing of God. Some have lost their blessings through demonic food eaten in dreams. It is also important that every word we utter from our mouth should edify the Holy Spirit and the body of Christ as we are living sacrifices, *holy*, and must be pleasing to God everywhere. *Some have lost their blessings through careless talk, uncontrollable anger and bitterness. Darkness and light cannot dwell together.*

6. 4 (iv) Prayer

Jesus prayed without ceasing until His death. At times some of His disciples felt too tired to pray. We cannot be tired to pray when we have received a *personal prophecy* that would destroy us or kill us.

With the knowledge that He was going to die, Jesus still prayed for hours. He gave a personal prophecy to Peter that he would deny Him three times (Matt. 26: 31–35). Why did He prophecy such about Peter? *Because He knew what would happen between the period He had the vision about Peter's denial and the would-be time of occurrence of the event. Peter was going to sleep instead of praying.* At Gethsemane He asked Peter, 'Could you men not keep watch with me for one hour? Watch and pray so that you will not fall into temptation. The spirit is willing, but the body is weak' (Matt. 26: 40–41). When it mattered most to pray, Peter and the two sons of Zebedee slept. As a result, Peter's flesh was weak when he denied Jesus three times. He did not join in prayer when it mattered most. Lack of personal prayer for himself allowed the *personal prophecy* to happen. But the Lord prayed for restoration, and again we saw Peter very prominent amongst the works and Acts of the Apostles in the New Testament. I say the Spirit of God is in us and willing to assist. Pray so that the flesh may be strong enough to resist the enemy when it matters most. The Word informs that we pray without ceasing with different petitions, different styles of prayer, in the open and in private. An ideal prayer is Matt. 6: 9–13.

6.4 (v) Praise and Worship

Ask the Lord to give you a personal revelation of the effect of Praise and Worship. Study Psalm 150 on Praise and Worship, and the effect of Praise and Worship at the battle of Jericho, through the blowing of Trumpets. Praise is the wind of heaven. Praise lightens every burden. The Lord must be praised; He loves it (Isaiah 150). His name is Praise, and His other name is Worship. That is why we worship the way we do. It flattens and smothers every burden, and that is just God. Only God must be praised: only God must be danced to. No other God! Do not dance to any other God but Me – the great I AM.

6. 4 (vi) Fasting

Some breakthroughs are achieved only through fasting. Moses and Jesus fasted for forty days and forty nights, Queen Esther asked the Jews to go without food and drink for three days and nights. What sort of fasting does the Lord desire? (see Isaiah 58). With the increase in the propensity to commit sin and depending on the situation, my personal prescription is to go on fasting indefinitely. Even the controllers and authorities of this world deliver, when prisoners and protesters go on hunger strike! How much more, the ever-faithful living God

Why fast indefinitely? I will explain with two examples using

6.0 The Prophecy Box Further Elaborated and Explained

Moses and the people of Israel, and Noah and those in the ark respectively[1]. It is possible we go onto the mountain of God for forty days and forty nights, and receive revelation promise and anointing from God. But the spiritual atonement to completely and swiftly release our blessings may take longer. The spiritual atonement of Israel was not completed in the first forty days; it was completed in eighty days. Then, the heart of Israel was spiritually clean, prepared and open to receive a new covenant relationship and key to their perfect blessings from God. Therefore, Moses' first forty days was not enough to atone for the sins of Israel (Exodus 31: 18–34: 28).

It took a period of over one year and more (375 days to be exact) in the presence and under the refuge of God for Noah and the selected creatures to step again on dry land after they were lifted into the heavens because of the forty days and forty nights destructive rain that ravaged the earth. God told Noah on the 17th day of the second month of the six hundredth year of his life, 'seven days from now I will send rain on the earth for forty days and forty nights, and I will wipe from the face of the earth every living creature I have made' (Gen. 7: 4). For seven days Noah prepared for the heavenly realms; all the selected creatures came to him. As rain fell Noah and the selected creatures inside the cover of God were lifted into the heavens, far above the mountains as the floodwater gates let loose. After the fortieth day of destruction by rain, the floodwater gates of hell started receding steadily under the omnipotent and omniscient power of God. Noah did not come out of the ark or the presence of God immediately. It took a time of watching and waiting upon the Holy Spirit, who closed the door of the ark to evil in the first place, to tell Noah when to actually open the windows for the raven and then the dove to check if the earth was safe enough again to live in, and for them to finally come out of the heavenly cover. It was a slow process descending from the heavens to dry surface, to see if the land of the living was fit enough to live in. After the first one hundred and fifty days (five months), it took another forty days waiting; series of seven days waiting and daily

---

[1] Note, I am not implying that Noah and those in the Ark fasted, I only intend to discuss a process that relates to how indefinite fasting becomes effective.

waiting in the presence of God before Noah and all the creatures left the presence of God. On the second occasion when the dove was sent out it returned in the evening. There in its beak was a peace symbol – a freshly plucked olive leaf. Then Noah knew as a sign from the Holy Spirit that the water had finally receded from the earth (sin had finally receded). It took 375 days in all before God said to Noah to come out of the ark; and that was exactly the 27th day of the second month of his six hundred and first year on earth. Noah then gave thanks to the Lord by building an altar to the Lord and sacrificed burnt offerings on it. The Lord liked the smell, and made a promise in His heart that never again would He curse the ground because of man's evil inclination (Genesis 7 and 8).

Effective fasting and the whole process described using Noah and those in the Ark are analogous to a minimum of 90 minutes soccer match where one of two teams must win. There are two soccer teams: (i) the Christian team and (ii) the Satanic (or the demonic) team. The forty days and forty nights that water ravaged the earth can be likened to a situation whereby the satanic team is freely scoring goals and is winning the soccer match. The tide changed in favour of the Christian team, and the spiritual attack and progress of the satanic team began to falter as the Ark began to descend. The time the Ark began to descend gradually and steadily from heaven can be likened to a time of increasingly effective continuous fasting powered by the Holy Ghost; striving for holiness; and the outpouring of God's anointing and grace upon the Christian team. The Christian team, therefore, began to counter-attack (slowly or speedily) and the demonic team began to recede backwards to protect their goalpost. Indefinite fasting (for example, continuous fasting) will put insurmountable pressure on the now defensive satanic team. As the Satanic team begin to lose their confidence and are not readily willing to be smote and smothered by the anointing of the Holy Ghost, the match may become fiercer at this stage. But, with the Holy Spirit-given gift-dynamics (for instance, fasting coupled with effective combination of specific deliverance ministration and warfare prayers), quality, excellent, admirable, noble and creative goals will easily become possible to score and victory will come in due season and exactly right on time before the soccer referee blows the final whistle. The awesomeness of victory will be as clear as the miraculous escape of the sole survivor of a plane crash.

As the examples have indicated, the high places and strongholds of Satan will be removed with indefinite fasting powered by the Holy Ghost.

Also, another fact to take hold of is that the speed at which reductive- prophecies recede and restoration and blessings take their place is slower in the physical realm than the immediate breakthrough we may have received in the spirit realm as we wait on God. It is important that the Counsellor gives us information about the exact time to disembark the spirit realm, and also energizes us and strengthens our inner man enough before we descend. So it is better we spend more time in the presence of God even if we have received our breakthrough in the spirit realm.

6.4 (vii) Healing and Deliverance

To what extent do Christian-believers enjoy the effective power and anointing of the Holy Spirit? There must be great joy if the Holy Spirit will reveal that which could occur in the future and it is possible to alter the course of unfavourable events. Contaminating evil spirits, such as the destructive spirits of sorrow, failure and accidents, are able to permeate the spirit realm (visions and dreams of Christian-believers) as a result of curses and sin. Though a Christian has experienced salvation and the gift of the Holy Spirit, he or she may not attain the optimum benefits of the power of the resurrection of Jesus Christ until the power of sin and curses (such as ancestral and generational curses and bondages) are broken in the Christian's life. Curses lead to spiritual oppression, humiliation, failure, unnecessary toil and struggles, and injustice by evil spirits. I will advise that every Christian should visit regularly deliverance and healing clinics, particularly those who notice undesirable patterns in their lives which they can also associate with their forebears. There are Christians and Ministers specially gifted with deliverance and healing anointing. Mountain of Fire and Miracles (MFM) Ministries with branches in several parts of the world is at the forefront of this engagement with the forces of darkness and *power must change hands* to the benefit of the Christian-believer. Very recently I have stressed deliverance and healing ministration to those close to me because of benefits I have obtained from deliverance and healing clinics I have visited; revelation knowledge from the Holy Spirit of undesirable patterns and designs in my life that needed to be strategically prayed about and broken; and finally, the continuous spiritual and physical release from bondages of old. Personally, I strongly believe for any Christian, deliverance and healing must be an on-going process, even when permanent blessings are witnessed in the physical realm. Most experienced and anointed deliverance Ministers I have met yet are those who were once severely oppressed by the enemy, and they do not take the ministration lightly.

I have noticed that most Christian-believers of affluent background and education tend to look down and disregard any form of deliverance and healing ministration. Most probably because the manifestations of deliverance or evil spirits leaving the body and casting out of demons are seen as not too comforting sights – horrible and un-admirable. Sometimes, I believe, some are denied their blessings as a result of this. Horrible and disgusting manifestations during ministration are better than living a substandard life. That believers might quickly enter into their blessings with minimum toil and struggle, casting out of demons was very important to the ministry of Jesus Christ in the New Testament. Demons were once driven out of Mary Magdalene the mother of James, a close associate of Jesus Christ who witnessed God in flesh in all His power, might and glory and accompanied Him from the early days of His ministry on earth. Demons are no respecters of Christian-believers; they must be continually cast out as Jesus Christ continually cast them out! I call on Ministers and Leaders to give adequate recognition to deliverance and healing clinics and ministries within their Fellowships and Churches. I revert again to Hosea 4: 6 which says, 'my people are destroyed by lack of knowledge. Because you have rejected knowledge, I also reject you as my priests…'

Furthermore, if the problems of witchcraft, manipulation of ancestral spirits, hereditary spirits and familial spirits were absent, the African, Africa and the rest of the developing world would know and enjoy more meaningful development in all spheres of life. Really, it is only the introduction of this religious and spiritual quotient and awareness into the understanding of the issues of development economics and into the deductive, intellectual and planning framework of world institutions like the United Nations, World Bank and other aid agencies and institutions would present endeavour, frustrations and limitations in the developing world be more understandable and well-guided. This is another study in itself beyond the scope of this study.

Holy standards and requirements of God (i) to (vii) are ways I would consider appropriate to deal with reductive-prophecies. I will also recommend that you read the A–Z Model of the Word.

6.5 WHEN WILL THERE BE AN END TO REDUCTION (DISCOMFORT, DISCOURAGEMENT, DECEPTION AND CONFLICT)?

There will be an end to *reduction* (discomfort, conflict, deception, anger, humiliation, pain etc.) at the end of our age on earth, when the Lord creates new heavens and a new earth. Prophet Isaiah captures the future with great eloquence. Study Isaiah 60 and 65. The Lord says in Isaiah 65: 17–25,

> Behold, I will create new heavens and a new earth. The former things will not be remembered, nor will they come to mind. But be glad and rejoice for ever in what I will create, for I will create Jerusalem to be a delight and its people a joy. I will rejoice over Jerusalem and take delight in my people; the sound of weeping and of crying will be heard in it no more. Never again will there be in it an infant who lives but a few days, or an old man who does not live out his years; he who dies at a hundred will be thought a mere youth; he who fails to reach a hundred will be considered accursed. They will build houses and dwell in them; they will plant vineyards and eat their fruit. No longer will they build houses and others live in them, or plant and others eat. For as the days of a tree, so will be the days of my people; my chosen ones will long enjoy the works of their hands. They will not toil in vain or bear children doomed to misfortune; for they will be a

people blessed by the Lord, they and their descendants with them. Before they call I will answer; while they are still speaking I will hear. The wolf and the lamb will feed together, and the lion will eat straw like the ox, but dust will be the serpent's food. They will neither harm nor destroy on all my holy mountain.'

New Testament books like Revelation could not improve on the language; they merely quoted Isaiah. Even part of the ideal prayer of Jesus (Matt. 6: 9–10) says, 'Our Father in heaven, hallowed be your name, your kingdom come, your will be done on earth as it is in heaven…' I personally believe it is still prayer and changes in our lifestyles that will bring about the prophesied new heavens and the new earth. Then God's zeal and faith in His word would now give the breakthrough.

In the new age every creation and situation will be in their rightful place. There would not be need for restoration and *personal prophecy* (our Adamic self would have been restored to the image of God). Everything will be in perfect harmony with the perfect image of our creator. Then we shall live and not experience death, like immortals who pleased God such as Enoch and Elijah. Between Noah and the end of the Old Testament was estimated to be two thousand years, and between the death of Jesus Christ and now is two thousand years.

Isaiah 66: 18 and 66: 22–24 says God would come soon.

Thus, *Prophecy* as revealed by the Word of God from Genesis to Revelation may sometimes be accompanied by *reduction* before *restoration* and then elevation.

Epilogue

The word of God is good news to the poor in spirit. Just as the blood of Jesus Christ drenched the depths of the earth with the experience of His crucifixion, so does the experience of resurrection make power available to win souls round the globe, round the clock. The Lord Jesus Christ completed the work of salvation two thousand years ago when He died for all mankind. Let us, therefore tap into the power of the blood and do the work of ministry, get involved in missions and become effective in the marketplace. We must *light* and *salt* the world.

A tragic defeat (that is *reduction*) in the book of Genesis was revealed to us when man, created in the very image of God, rebelled through the experience of Adam and Eve with the serpent. The book of Revelation ends with a reunion (that is *restoration*) as it reveals, and there is a blessed ending after all[1]. To restore man back to the ideal state before his rebellion is the ultimate plan of God for man. To live in paradise is God's wish; and for His glorification is His mandate for mankind. We must therefore pray and bring the heavens down. First, we must take authority of the spirit realm and then things will begin to change in the physical realm – in the real world where we live.

With the present decadence and all forms of *reduction* in the world we live in, it is still the plan of God that *restoration* will follow reduction. As sad as the incidents on 9/11, in Dunblane, Scotland may seem, there will be *restoration*. With the humiliation and killing of millions of Jews by the Nazis in the Second World War, who ever thought the nation of Israel would be created so soon in 1948? Three years after the Second World War, the esteem of the Jews was already being *restored* in the land of the living. What about the incarceration and reduction of Nelson

---

[1] 'A Happy Ending After all' in *The NIV Insight Bible*, Hodder & Stoughton, London, p.1114.

Mandela for over two decades and the killings in the South African townships? Who would ever have thought that Mandela despite his *reduction* and humiliation by the apartheid regime would ever be *restored* and rule the *rainbow* country, and that there would ever be some 'peace' in the black townships?

God is God and His sovereignty remains in our dark world. The earth remains the Lord's, and those the Lord's Hand rest upon, they shall be *restored*, fortified and never be afraid. As the Psalmists wrote, 'The earth is the Lord's, and everything in it, the world, and all who live in it; for He established it upon the seas and established it upon the waters' (Psalm 24: 1–2), and also, 'Those who trust in the Lord are like Mount Zion, which cannot be shaken but endures forever. As the mountains surround Jerusalem so the Lord surrounds His people both now and forever. The sceptre of the wicked will not remain over the land allotted to the righteous, for then the righteous may use their hands to do evil' (psalm 125: 1–3).

What is the solution to the decadence (particularly prevalent moral decadence) of this dark world? The gospel of peace of our Lord Jesus Christ remains the only solution to the real issues of society. The answer is not in the hands of the politicians, nor the economists. The gospel of peace of Jesus Christ is not only spiritually absolute in today's world, but also politically, socially and economically absolute and very relevant.

Our security as creations of God is only in God. Our security as Christians and the security of *Israel* is in God almighty and not otherwise. Our true peace and only peace is in Jesus Christ. Christianity must leave the terrain of compartmentalization and be overwhelmingly relevant in all facets and commanding heights of society: Christians must assume the role of servants to society[1]. For this to occur in the not-too-distant future (as it was some time ago) I am tempted to say we as Christian-believers and the nation of Israel still have the key – for ours and theirs are the prosperity assured by the psalmists.

As the Jews can be considered as the model of the adversities of man (or what could plague a people), they are still a model of

---

[1] 'The Church as Servant' in *Models of the Church*, Avery Dulles, Gill and Macmillan Press Ltd., 1987, pp.89 –102.

Epilogue

the kind of blessings with which God can also endow a people. For no other people were as fortunate and blessed as Israel was, as revealed in the Old Testament, and so it must be today with New Testament believers, particularly with those whom God's Hands are upon. As we serve a consistent God, the nation of *Israel* must come back to God and acknowledge His Son as Lord and Saviour. As it was in biblical times and is still is today, *Israel* is still strategic in the plans of God for the world and the nations, and in claiming back the wealth of nations back to the kingdom of God. For all things were created by Him, and He has given accordingly to His first-born and all His own. For I am always tempted to say no other people are as blessed as *Israel*.

Believers must own the world. The blessings of God are not far off. They are still predominantly with those He established the first covenant with. No one is more fortunate than Israel and His seed, with which the Lord established the first covenant. And the Lord will not forget His first seed and the covenant He established ages past, O Ancient of Days which is like yesterday to Him, but a long time forgotten by men. In harnessing the wealth of the earth and of the nations back to God and His chosen, the nation of Israel would need to retrace her steps back to God and acknowledge Jesus Christ as Lord and sovereign. Israel must come back to God and Jerusalem (the city of David and our God) must remain secure and one, and at the heart of Israel and not shared.

For this the Prophets tenaciously craved; of this Jesus Christ spoke; of this the Apostle St. Paul and John the Baptist expounded; for this Jesus Christ left the Holy Spirit. Bringing back *Israel*, the world and all her fortune to Jesus Christ is what we as Christian-believers and children of God (co-inheritants) must strive and crave for in ministry, mission and the marketplace (for instance, in ship owning, trading, banking and finance, oil and gas, high tech, and all commanding heights of society) until the day of our Lord Jesus Christ. We must light and salt the world. Our impact must be felt in all sectors and humanist professions. The fortune of the world and His entire creation must rest in the house of God.

The Word is Prophecy God is God and His sovereignty remains in a dark world.

Bibliography

The following books influenced my thought during the period of writing this book:

Brueggeman, Walter, *The Prophetic Imagination*, USA, Fortress Press, 1978

Colson, Charles W. with Ellen Santilli Vaughn, *Unity of the Church. Being light in darkness*, London, Word Publishing, 1992

Dulles, Avery, *Models of the Church*, Gill and Macmillan Press Ltd., 2nd Edition, 1987

Green, L., *Let's do Theology*, London, Mowbray, 1990

Grudem, Wayne, *Systematic Theology. An Introduction to Biblical Doctrine*, England, Inter-Varsity Press and USA: Zodervan Publishing House, 1994: 1016–1088

Harper Collins Publishers, *Collins English Dictionary*, Major New Edition, 1991

Hodder & Stoughton, *The Insight Bible, NIV*: Notes by Philip Yancey and Tim Stafford, 1992

www.ingramcontent.com/pod-product-compliance
Lightning Source LLC
LaVergne TN
LVHW041536060526
838200LV00037B/1007